WITHIN the STILLNESS

WITHIN

the STILLNESS

One Family's Winter on a Northern Trapline

Keith Olsen

Your Nickel's Worth Publishing
Regina, SK.

Within the Stillness: One Family's Winter on a Northern Trapline

Library and Archives Canada Cataloguing in Publication

Olsen, Keith, 1960-
Within the stillness : one family's winter on a northern trapline / Keith Olsen.

ISBN 978-1-894431-61-3

1. Olsen, Keith, 1960-. 2. Olsen, Keith, 1960- —Family.
3. Outdoor life—Saskatchewan, Northern. 4. Wilderness survival—Saskatchewan, Northern.
5. Cree Indians—Saskatchewan, Northern—Biography. 6. Saskatchewan, Northern—Biography.
I. Title.

FC3543.25.O57A3 2011 971.24'103092 C2011-902161-7

Layout and design by Heather Nickel
Cover and frontispiece image of Mahigan River © Keith Olsen
All photos © Olsen Family Collection

Printed in Canada
April 2011

FSC
www.fsc.org
MIX
Paper from responsible sources
FSC® C016245

ENVIRONMENTAL BENEFITS STATEMENT

Your Nickel's Worth Publishing saved the following resources by printing the pages of this book on chlorine free paper made with 100% post-consumer waste.

TREES	WATER	SOLID WASTE	GREENHOUSE GASES
8 FULLY GROWN	3,850 GALLONS	234 POUNDS	799 POUNDS

Calculations based on research by Environmental Defense and the Paper Task Force.
Manufactured at Friesens Corporation

Your Nickel's Worth Publishing
Regina, SK.

www.yournickelsworth.com

For my wife, Joan

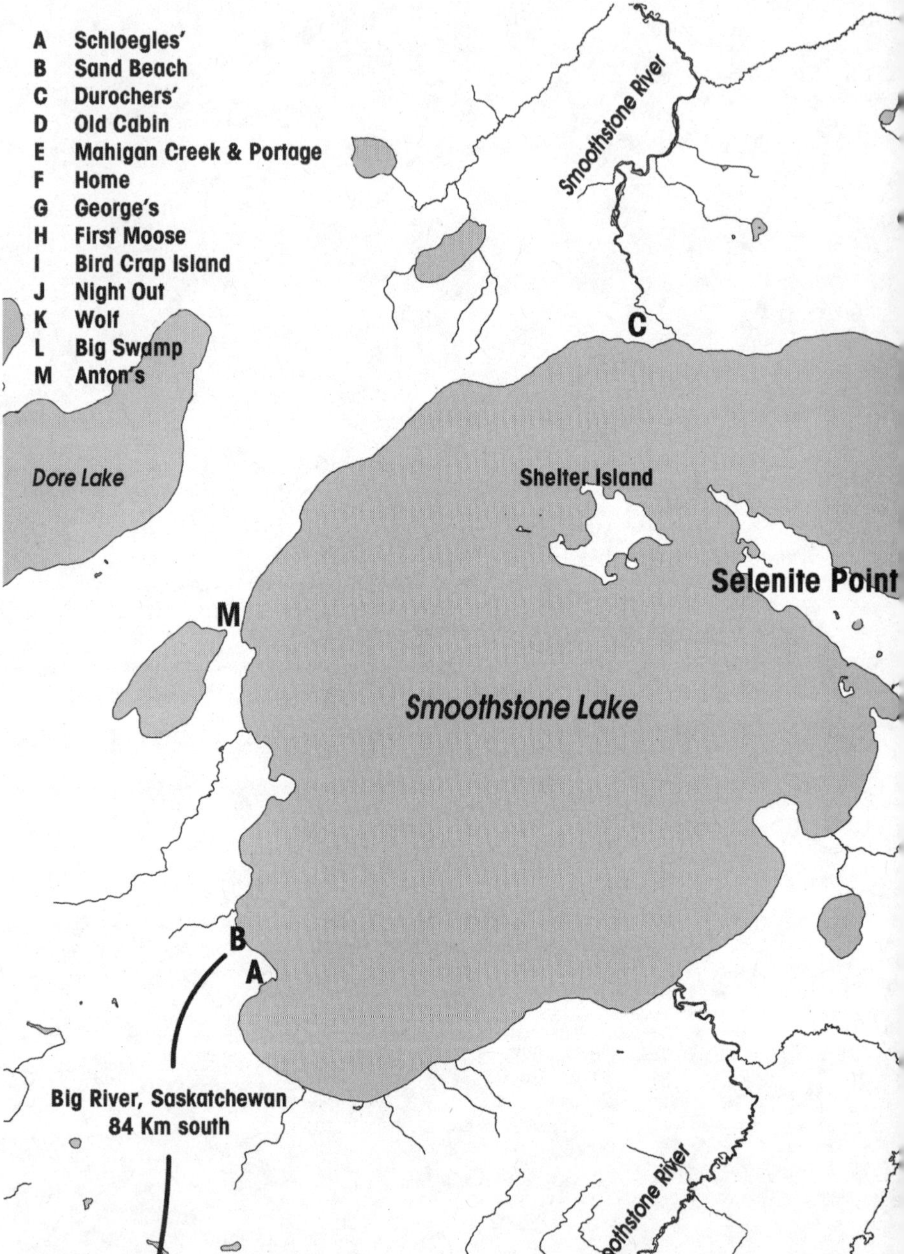

A Schloegles'
B Sand Beach
C Durochers'
D Old Cabin
E Mahigan Creek & Portage
F Home
G George's
H First Moose
I Bird Crap Island
J Night Out
K Wolf
L Big Swamp
M Anton's
Smoothstone River
Dore Lake
Shelter Island
Selenite Point
Smoothstone Lake
M
C
B
A
Big River, Saskatchewan
84 Km south
Smoothstone River

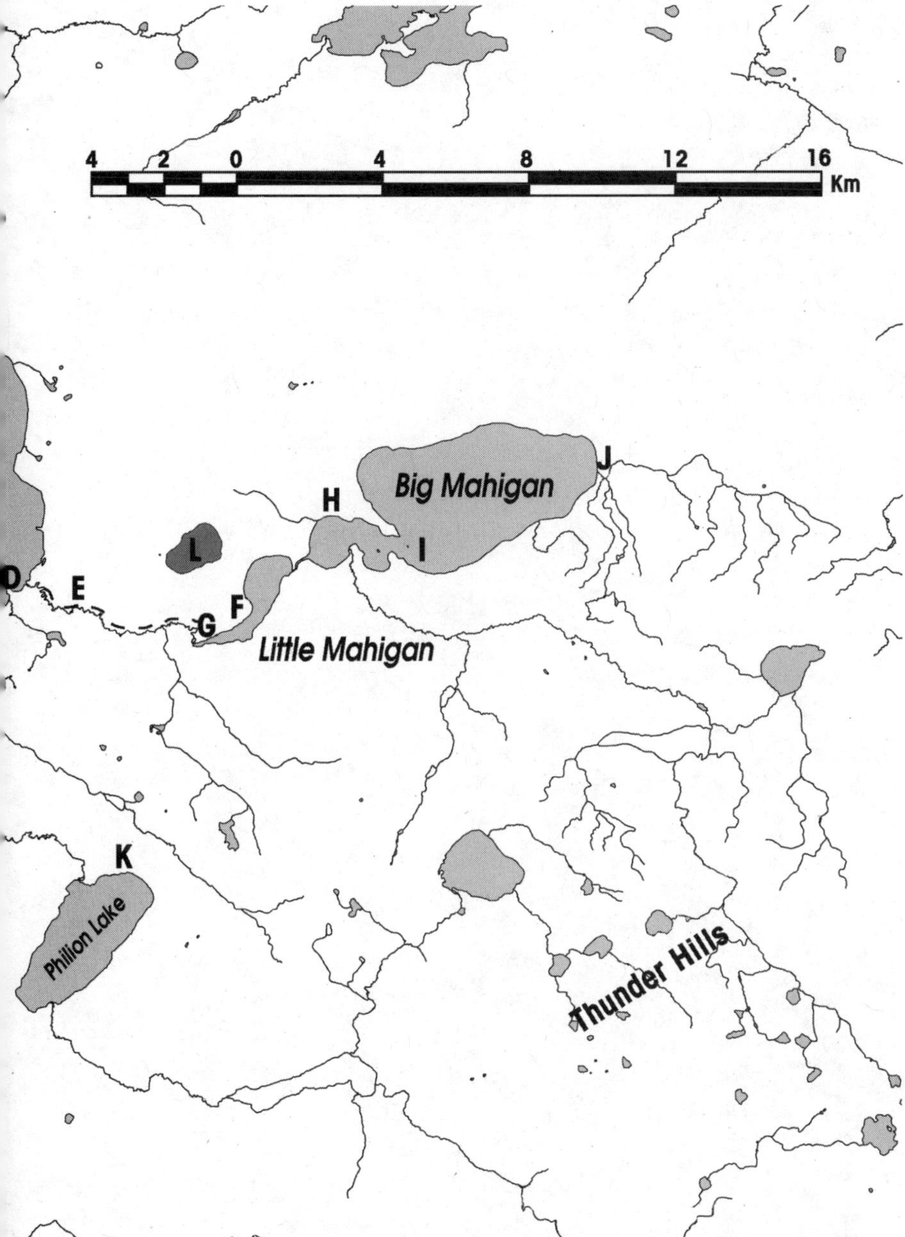
4
2
0
4
8
12
16
Km
Big Mahigan
J
H
I
L
D
E
F
G
Little Mahigan
K
Philion Lake
Thunder Hills

"Within you there is a stillness and a sanctuary
to which you can retreat at any time and be yourself."

Hermann Hesse

reflection

Driving across a small wooden bridge we approached a large gravel pit. In the centre were a couple of large stockpiles of gravel the logging companies used for the road. We turned in and drove a short distance between the stockpiles until we found a flat surface to park on. Clarence and I stepped out of his one-ton truck and walked the perimeter of the pit, hoping to find the access point to the old portage. After a brief survey of the area we noticed what seemed to be the opening; it was almost hidden by a pile of gravel that had been pushed in front. On closer inspection we saw it was indeed a trail—a well-used one at that. The wheel tracks of a quad, a type of four-wheel motor bike, had worn small ruts into the ground.

Without hesitation we broke into a swift walk and followed the trail. It worked its way through the long-standing poplar trees and smaller underbrush. Though it wasn't the original portage, our excitement grew as the tracks turned south towards the river. The narrow trail was in great condition and we made excellent time, soon finding what looked like the old overland

End of the portage

portage and following it. It wasn't long before we could see parts of the river through the bush and already we could hear a lot of activity on the water. Once we got close enough the commotion was revealed to be a flock of geese, some waterfowl and whole lot of large adult pelicans drying themselves along the grassy bank.

When we got to a little knoll near the river they spotted us and there was mayhem. They all took off at once, geese mixed in with pelicans and even a few ducks thrown in for good measure. It was a comedy of squawking. Despite the level of noise and the effort they made to escape, they flew only a little distance, just as far as the next bend in the river where they landed and carried on about their business. And we continued on as well, down the old path with a considerable amount of enthusiasm, knowing we were on the old portage once again.

We recognized the trail by old stumps among the trees; they had been hewn down alongside the corridor of the portage, possibly to remove deadfall across the trail or if they were dry, for use as firewood. The trail led through large stands of mature Jack pine, following along the bank of the river. The blue sky was crystal clear, warm for an early spring day, and the river gurgled softly as it flowed steadily downstream.

All of this we found nostalgic and intoxicating.

The quad tracks made a quick detour to a hunting blind someone had set up for last fall's deer hunt. From this point on there were no more signs of machinery. The portage was still clearly visible, though, now a worn-down game trail that randomly tunneled its way through the bush. We climbed over a few fallen trees and through heavier underbrush layered in a thick blanket of green moss. A poplar bluff stood sentry at the end of this corridor, its majestic trees guarding the trail, doing their best to withstand the passage of time. A few of these monsters had lost the battle and sprawled across the ground like fallen soldiers. Still, they were useful as compost—nothing is wasted in nature.

Through this stand of poplar was smaller growth made up of birch trees and alder willow. We could sense an opening by the sound of the wind blowing through the forest and then—with one last corner—the lake.

Memories flooded in and time stood still. All was quiet. No words were spoken. Our thoughts turned back to another era, an almost-forgotten distant past. Standing there on the shoreline of Mahigan Lake we reflected on the events of forty-five years earlier...

a time before

As always, there was ample opportunity for reminiscing. Dad sat down with a cup of hot tea in his hands and related the story of when he'd first brought Mum to Mahigan Lake. There are two linked lakes bearing this name, a smaller one and a larger one, and it was on the west shore of Little Mahigan that Dad and Mum wanted to live.

By 1957, Dad'd had enough of the mink ranch scene at Egg Lake near La Ronge and needed to get back to the familiar territory of his childhood. He and Mum made their way to Big River, staying for a few months before continuing northwards for a visit with Anton Mylengar at Smoothstone Lake. These visits continued over the next few years while Clarence and I were born. It was in the late summer of 1960 that Dad decided to make a trip to Mahigan. At the time, Clarence and I were small and real bundles of joy, so our folks left us in Big River in Grandma Florence's more-than-capable hands.

After arriving at the big lake, Anton Mylengar transported them across by boat to the old cabin at Selenite Point where

Dad had once lived with his grandfather. Anton was left with the instruction to pick them up in a month. It took them a few days to settle in and make it feel like home. Dad was anxious to scout the old country in hopes of finding a likely spot to set up a permanent residence. He planned on trapping, and set off to search the area to see if this venture was viable and could sustain a family. The fur trade was on the rise again and the upcoming trapping season looked very promising. The price of fur had increased; so too had the demand for northern pelts. But life up north was still very hard and any opportunity to make a better living was certainly worth investigating.

Dad and Mum at Mahigan Lake

After a short spell at Selenite, Dad's patience wore thin and the need to move on grew from an itch to a necessity. After an early breakfast and under clear skies they left Selenite Point for Mahigan across the old and familiar overland portage. My parents were youthful, energetic and in great shape. They covered the ground at a fair pace and soon found themselves halfway through the portage where the trail led them onto a grassy knoll alongside the river. It seemed almost a duty to stop for tea and a bit of lunch at this spot. It was late summer and very pleasant out—there were only a very few of the pesky insects that thrive along the river and marshland.

They continued on and before long reached the end of the

trail and the shoreline of Mahigan Lake. This was a great spot to spend the night, so Dad suggested that Mum set up a temporary camp in among the deadfall and start a fire. Meanwhile, he'd go further up the lake to see if there was a more likely spot to make camp. He took his rifle along in hopes of bagging a moose and told Mum he'd be back soon.

Mum chopped a few branches to clear a spot for the bedding, then gathered a few smaller stones from along the edge of the shore to form the firepit. Sounds of splashing echoed across the lake where several moose waded along the far shore. It was a little early for rutting season, but the moose gave the odd bellow.

There was no wind and the skies remained clear. Not a cloud to be seen. The blue of the sky slowly deepened as the day wore on. Maybe this heralded the unseen change in season because in place of the tranquil summer's eve Mum had anticipated, there was an inordinate amount of noise: ducks flapping and squawking, the high-pitched shriek of some marsh hawk on the hunt, and the ongoing saga of the moose across the water.

And then—a gunshot!

From somewhere up the shore its echo rolled down the lake and across the hills until the thick forest swallowed it up. For a moment there was sharp silence; everything stilled as if expecting something more. But nothing came and no more was heard. Soon the early twilight was again alive with flapping, squawking and shrieking, although after the sudden quiet the cacophony seemed louder than before.

By now it was getting late in the day. Mum was about to light the campfire when she heard the loud crack of a nearby branch. She looked up to meet the gaze of a huge bull moose. It was just a few feet away and it was enormous.

Mum froze! She wanted to scream but nothing would come out and after a suspended moment that felt like an eternity she gathered enough courage to make a dive for the windfalls where she'd laid the bedding for the night. Dad had told her there were moose all over the place, but she'd rather thought he was trying to scare her so hadn't taken him too seriously. Now, however, she was firmly convinced that it was no tall tale—she'd never seen a specimen like this one!

She thought hard about what she should do and recalled being told that when confronted with a moose—and what a moose!—she should get in among heavy trees or down into the deadfall like she was now. As secure as she could be for the moment, she stayed put. Uncertain whether or not yelling at the moose would be a good thing and worried that doing so might draw antagonistic attention to her, she hunkered down and stayed quiet. The moose soon grew bored and ambled on down into the lake where it wandered off, splashing through the water and making deep-chested, guttural grunts, contributing a considerable amount to the volume of the already noisy neighbourhood.

Nightfall was fast approaching and there was still no sign of Dad. Mum was now becoming really scared and didn't dare move from the shelter. As the last light faded from the sky, Dad emerged from the forest to Mum's overwhelming relief. He called out to see where she was—he'd thought the fire would be going and the tea already on. He had a moment of panic thinking perhaps something had happened, but the thought was short-lived. Mum popped out of the makeshift shelter and quickly explained the moose encounter.

Dad had a story to tell as well. After he'd left Mum to set up camp, he'd walked about a mile north along the shoreline when he came across a yearling calf moose wading along the shore. After he shot the moose, an enraged cow came crashing out of the bush, charging him repeatedly and keeping him pinned down in some large trees. This continued on well into the afternoon but Dad had no desire to shoot the cow moose as well. He was surprised at the ferocity of the animal—her actions were far beyond normal, especially since the calf should have been weaned. Eventually, though, the cow left and Dad had been able to butcher the young animal.

Now that he was back they were able to finish preparing the campsite and start a fire. With a good, hot blaze the teapot was soon boiling and fresh moose tenderloin, skewered on a stick, set to roast over the fire. This made for a great, although very late, evening meal. Afterwards, they sat watching the glowing coals die down into black lumps of charcoal. Dad spoke again of the tremendous number of moose in the area and this time there was no argument from Mum; she was in total agreement!

Having a moose stare you down is not a regular occurrence, let alone twice in the same day—maybe it was a sign, a portent that there'd be an opportunity to set up an outfitting camp in the future. Regardless, safe and with full bellies, it was time to turn in for the night. They lay listening to the final snap and crack of the dying embers from the firepit as it cooled down and the slow hush of nature settle in all around. The bed was excellent and being real tired it was not long before sleep overtook them—and with it dreams of what tomorrow would bring.

The next few days were taken up with the chores of drying meat and scouting the rest of the area around the lake. Finding a suitable place from which to prepare a future building site wasn't difficult. The chosen spot was about a mile north of the portage on the west shore, about halfway up the lake in a small clearing among a stand of tall Jack pine where the shoreline rounded to form a shallow point. It immediately felt like home and soon become the base for all other activities. Plans were made to build their future home on this spot.

Four weeks later, the dry meat was prepared, the scouting finished, and there was no further need to stay. Besides, they had an overwhelming desire to see their children. It was time to head back to the outside world.

building our home

It was early summer when we drove up to Smoothstone Lake with a truckload of our belongings. Dad had chartered an airplane out of La Ronge to meet us at the big sand beach. From there it would fly us and our gear into Mahigan Lake. The aircraft was a red, low-winged Beechcraft on pontoons with two small, round tailfins at the back. It had two engines, one on each wing. It made a couple of trips into Mahigan with our gear before taking us. Each trip the plane was well loaded down with material, equipment and our grubstake for the summer. It even took our wood freighter canoe tied securely underneath between the struts.

Dad had made an earlier arrangement to have our other canoe delivered to the portage; we would need it to come back across Smoothstone later in the summer. After we had arrived at Mahigan, our first task was to erect a small structure called a shack-tent—a wood frame complete with pole rafters, a plywood floor and a single row of plywood around the exterior for walls. This was then covered over with a canvas prospector's tent.

The shack-tent was very small in size—only eight by ten feet—but it filled our immediate need for shelter. It was just a temporary living arrangement while the main cabin was being built. There was enough room inside for two beds: a small bed at the back for us boys and another along the side wall for Mum and Dad. Near the front entrance was a tiny kitchen table and a small, metal airtight stove for heat. These little oval stoves were made of light gauge steel and were therefore inexpensive, making them perfect for this sort of use. A gas lantern provided light in the evening and sometimes a bit of heat, but it was used sparingly to conserve fuel. Mostly we used the coal oil lamp or wax candles for general lighting.

The main cabin was built square, twenty by twenty, and constructed with horizontal logs, six high. It was finished off with two-by-four uprights above the logs and sheathed with exterior plywood. The interior floor was made out of log floor beams and two-by-six lumber joists covered over with sawn wood planks. The roof had log support beams spaced two feet apart sheathed over with the same material used for the floor. The roof was weatherproofed with roll roofing. Inside, the upper part of the walls were insulated and covered over with plywood. Dad put six windows in the cabin facing east towards the lake. Our source of heat came from a forty-five gallon barrel made into a stove and it stood upright in the middle of the southwest side of the new cabin.

One of the camp rules—which became a source of evening entertainment and a treasured highlight of our time there—was that at a scheduled hour each day all building and any form of activity resulting noise would stop. This rule allowed stillness to settle and bring peace and solitude to our surroundings. And

Dad at our new home on Little Mahigan Lake

we didn't have to wait long before the sounds of nature came to life. One of the misconceptions of being in the bush is that it is all too quiet and you don't hear anything, but the truth of the matter is there is an orchestra of sounds in the deafening silence and a multitude of musicians waiting to be heard. Dad enforced this rule and it taught us both respect for nature and the ability to share it with the wildlife around us; when we were still, wildlife and waterfowl alike were given the opportunity to go about their activities undisturbed and unthreatened.

Another favourite activity was watching big game animals emerge from the forest to feed and drink along the lakeshore. There was always an abundance of white-tailed deer to be seen during the late afternoon. And as the evening progressed, moose would wade out into the lake until just their heads showed and feed on the green weeds growing up from the bottom, putting their heads under the surface until they were completely submerged, only to pop up with a loud snort and accompanying spray of water and weeds. My brother and I loved to watch the bull moose in all the grandeur of their magnificent sets of horns. A few black bears would, on occasion, show themselves when they came down to drink but they never stayed very long before disappearing back into the undergrowth.

Mahigan is the Cree name for "wolf." The lake is aptly named for the area's great number of these fierce canines and they didn't hesitate to let everyone know it. Oftentimes we enjoyed listening to their long, lonesome chorus and many nights it was the last thing we heard when the day came to a close.

The cabin itself took the better part of summer to complete. Spruce logs were taken from trees a short distance from the cabin's building site. Dad would pick out a tree of the right size and length—it had to be uniform from top to bottom—and eye it up to see if it was straight before cutting it down. Trees were randomly selected to thin out the treeline and underbrush, and strike the right balance between visibility and protection in case of fire. Once the tree was cut down and limbed, it was measured to the right length and cut. Dad packed the log on his shoulder to the building site, where he set it on a couple of sawhorses to remove the bark, which was peeled off with a draw knife. After the logs had been peeled they were set aside for drying. The trees were cut early enough in the season that the outer bark still peeled off with relative ease. Mum was thankful for that, as a fair amount of the peeling was left for her. When the cabin was completed and things were in order for the coming winter, we moved all our belongings in and left very little in the shack-tent.

After all the equipment was secure, we left for Big River where we stayed for several days. It was a busy time, visiting family, friends and gathering all the necessities for the coming winter at Mahigan Lake. This in itself was not an easy task because the trip out required the extra effort of taking the outboard motor, which had to be transported through the long overland portage. It was a huge undertaking to get it across the almost five-mile portage, but we needed it for the canoe waiting for us on the other end. So without anything further and everyone looking forward to the trip out, we were on our way.

the journey begins

It was early October and the afternoon was still very mild for the time of year—even the leaves weren't making any effort to fall from the branch. The wind and wet weather normally associated with the fall hadn't materialized nor were they even mentioned in the forecast. It was one of those seasons that seldom comes around and is known as late fall.

We were still in Big River and Dad was getting anxious to be on our way. That time of year always brings a real sense of urgency, the need to get going, knowing there is very little time to settle in before the lakes freeze over. Even the late fall and delayed freeze-up due to the warm weather didn't ease his desire to get an early start. And so we gathered everything we needed to sustain us over freeze-up and see us through the early stages of winter at Little Mahigan Lake.

The early light showed great promise of another good day. The sky was clear and the wind calm. Now that our return trip had started, we hoped it would stay that way. With all the personal items packed along with our gear, we loaded up the half-ton truck and made ready for the road trip into Smoothstone Lake. After a pit stop at the local gas station in Big River we were off, travelling north on a narrow gravel road for the fifty-mile trip into Smoothstone. The trip itself was uneventful, other than my brother and I getting bounced around in the truck when the tires found their fair share of potholes. Because the weather was so mild, the road surface was dry and covered in a fine powder of sand. The dust kicked up by the truck lingered in the air long after we passed and hung suspended like a heavy white fog. It was a good thing there was no traffic because it would've been a real problem meeting someone—or following behind them, for that matter.

It took us two hours to reach the landing at Smoothstone Lake. We pulled in alongside the beautiful sand beach, following a narrow road just wide enough for the truck. It led up to some buildings where the Schloegle family lived. Frank and Rosella and their five children—Louie, Ruth, John, Brenda and Barb—had moved here to the southwest shore of Smoothstone Lake from the farm. It was here our method of transportation would change from land vehicle to watercraft. The truck would stay here until our return and we would continue the journey to Little Mahigan in our narrow stern canoe.

Smoothstone Lake is basically a large open body of water, oval in shape and several miles across. The weather had held just fine and would make our crossing enjoyable. After a short visit with friends and a welcomed meal, we hauled all our gear and necessities down to the lake and loaded it into the canoe. With a last look around and a farewell wave we turned our attention to the far shoreline.

The canoe was powered by a five horsepower outboard motor and even with the generous load it pushed the craft quite nicely and soon the beach behind us receded into the distance. And like true northerners, there was no looking back; we were focussed on what lay ahead.

There was a very light wind coming from the north, just enough to put a ripple on the surface of the water, and as we headed into the wind we could feel a coolness begin to settle in—a reminder that the delayed change in weather was imminent and it was high time our path took us in the direction of winter camp.

We had one stop to make on the way in. On the very north shore near the mouth of Smoothstone River was the home of a wonderful couple, the Durochers. It was always a highlight in our travels to stop for a visit and it wasn't long before their camp came into view and Dad aimed the canoe towards the structures that made up their residence. We were a short distance away when we saw them come out of their cabin and start down towards the lake to meet us. Their sled dogs were making such a fuss on their way to the dock they could even be heard over the roar of the outboard motor! The Durochers worked them as a dog team during the winter months and kept them as pets in the summer, a vacation of sorts.

With the motor switched off, the canoe glided into the willing hands of these bush dwellers. Baptise Durocher—nicknamed "Caribou," for he could walk for miles—was a small, thin rail of a man, very nimble. With the expertise of long practice he quickly secured our canoe. And alongside him was his wife, Christine. We called her Mrs. Caribou. She was a short, robust woman, loud and full of laughter. It wasn't long before she had us boys out of the canoe and into a bear hug, all the while smothering us with an onslaught of kisses and incoherent baby talk—probably missing her own children who were in school at the time.

Amid the joyous greetings, customary handshakes, and the hugs and kisses, we were whisked off for the short climb to the cabin for tea and a meal from a fresh pot of stew that Mrs. Caribou had simmering on the fire outside. The afternoon stayed nice and warm, so we had lunch by the firepit. Caribou had made seats out of a large log he had sawn in half, with large blocks of wood for support. These two seats around the firepit made a great place to sit and have lunch. The chairs came with a personal guarantee they would not break and were well dried so you didn't have to worry about sap getting stuck to your bottom!

A tipi had been made into a drying rack, and Mrs. Caribou had a number of whitefish hanging from the racks above a slow-burning fire. The fish were getting a light smoke, drying and cooking all at the same time. This type of preparation is excellent as you can have a variety of meals with the dried fish and it still retains all the protein and nutrients. And once the fish has gone through this method of curing, it keeps for many days.

We would be spending the night with the Durochers and leaving for Mahigan in the morning. As the afternoon wore on it was time to get our sleeping gear out of the canoe so that Mum and Christine could make up the beds in the cabin. Then it was back outside for hot tea, bannock and homemade blueberry sauce—with lots of sugar for sweetening, just the way we two boys liked it. The adults' conversation lasted well into the evening and covered many topics, but the talk always came back to trapping and what lay ahead for the winter—especially the speculation of when freeze-up would occur and how long it would be before it happened. We all hoped that when the cold weather came it wouldn't snow right away. This would allow the lakes and muskegs to freeze over and make it safe for travelling.

Christine and Baptiste (Caribou) Durocher

There is a noticeable difference in the length of daylight at this time of year and, even though it was clear, darkness had settled in rather quickly. With a big day ahead and the long portage still to cross, we turned in early.

The last rays of sunlight on the horizon disappeared far behind the shoreline of Smoothstone, Dore Lake and into the distance beyond; it was time for dreams to take over—dreams of all the challenges and new adventures that lay ahead.

the durochers

The barking of the sled dogs woke us. Whether they'd heard something or not, once one started, all joined in the ruckus; it was their way of letting everyone know it was time to get the day underway, and, more importantly, to feed them! Sure enough, there was movement inside the cabin, and with a little groaning and after a few choice words regarding the barking dogs, there came a flurry of activity. Everyone seemed to get up at once and it was soon time to move out of the cabin for a stretch and a few gulps of crisp morning air.

A real chill had settled in during the night so building a fire became the morning's first priority. The firepit's flames had long since burned out, but fortunately there were enough live coals under the blanket of ash to get the fire going again. While Dad took on the chore of bringing in wood from the nearby woodpile, Caribou stirred the coals and added pieces of birchbark into the mix. He blew on the small pile of hot embers and soon had a flame started. To this he added kindling and topped it off with chunks of larger wood until he had a roaring fire.

Meantime, Mum shook out our bedding and tucked it back into our bags. All our personal items were taken down to the canoe and made ready for travel. Christine was bustling about, her small, round frame rushing back and forth preparing breakfast for us before we left. She took down a slab of bacon and trimmed off a few generous slices to fry in the large cast iron pan, already spitting hot on the fire her husband had made. She took out powdered eggs and mixed a bit of lake water in a tin to make batter for scrambled eggs. In another bowl, she added flour and baking powder to some of the egg mix for pancakes. Shortly, the air was filled with the sweet aroma of breakfast underway, and with great anticipation we looked forward to the morning meal. There's always something special about having a well-cooked, piping hot meal outdoors and it was no different then. Scrambled eggs, crispy sliced bacon, pancakes covered in hot blueberry sauce along with fried bannock and sweet tea—a great way to put a smile on your face and welcome a new day!

That morning the lake was exceptionally still for such a large body of water. There was a layer of dense white fog hovering over the surface like a blanket and when the sun rose above the eastern shore it was like turning on a massive fluorescent bulb. The heat from the sun slowly warmed the air, causing the fog to lift in millions of dancing lights like sparkling diamonds in the sky. It was a breathtaking sunrise. Once the fog bank started to move it didn't take long before it dissipated altogether and we could see Selenite Point across the way.

Selenite Point is a long peninsula of land stretching forward into Smoothstone Lake from the northeastern shore. It is about five miles in length and most of it is a mile wide until you near the tip, where it is just under a half-mile across. West and a bit south from the end of Selenite Point is a large island called Shelter Island. It is about a mile from the mainland and roughly a mile wide, running east to west, and two miles in length. From Caribou's vantage point, the island blended into the background and merged together with the point, making it look like Selenite Point extended out further than it really did.

The disappearance of the fog was the signal to say goodbye to the Durochers and we clambered once more into the canoe. Dad wound the pull cord around the fly wheel of the old Viking five- horse and with a quick jerk brought it to life with a small roar that was really more of a whine. *Whing-ing-ing. Put-put-put* and we were off, the canoe pointed in the direction of Selenite Bay, the portage and Mahigan.

We headed east along the north shore for a bit before angling south across to Selenite Point. Dad wanted to check on the old cabin where he'd once lived with his grandfather along the north shore of the point. It was close to the small river where the portage started and so was not out of our way. He wanted to see if anyone had been around, out of curiosity no doubt. It was a brief ride across and soon we paralleled the shoreline near the site where the old cabin stood. We didn't stop; in slowing down we could see that no one had been there for some time—the path that led up to the log cabin was overgrown with tall grass, thorn bushes and a multitude of weeds, mostly nettles.

On we went. Soon we could see the mouth of Mahigan River where it flowed into Smoothstone. Dad switched off the small outboard and used paddles to navigate the tiny stream. It was a short distance upstream to where we would land and begin the portage. This area of the lake is very shallow and the bank extends a fair distance out in the form of a grassy plain. Soft, bog-like hummocks dotted the field of muskeg, and as the water deepened tall bulrushes took over, the large black cattails swaying in the breeze. After briefly using the paddles to push our way up we came to the landing and, with a final shove, coasted in and came to a complete stop. Mum stepped out and held the canoe while Dad got out. He pulled the canoe further up the slight incline until it was stable and secure before allowing us boys to get out.

Once the gear and staples were taken out of the canoe, the craft was pulled completely out of the water and stored until further use. Dad had fastened poles to some trees about five feet above ground for the canoe to rest on. This helped keep the canoe dry and small rodents from chewing holes through the canvas. It also helped protect the craft from the curiosity of any wandering black bear. By hanging the canoe this way, the animal could see there was nothing available to eat inside and hopefully would leave the canoe alone.

The outboard was taken off for the return trip. Because we weren't able to take all the gear and staples in one trip, the items of priority would go in first, so everything was sorted and made ready for the five-mile journey into Little Mahigan Lake. Non-perishables remained behind and would be picked up at a later date. These were placed in a tree cache high enough above the ground to protect them from animals and covered over with a securely fastened tarpaulin to protect the contents from the elements. Dad made two travois, small A-frames constructed of little poles that would carry our belongings and the outboard motor. These were pulled by a rope made into a harness that rested on the shoulders. Our bedrolls were tied down in such a way that we were able to rest on them when we got tired of walking...not likely! Mum and Dad *must've* been adventuresome; I was just five and my brother Clarence, seven.

But before sorting what was to stay and what we'd bring to Mahigan by travois, Dad built a fire in the stone pit on the bank along the stream. While he organized what needed to go on this first trip Mum worked at getting lunch ready. She had tea on and heated the sandwiches Mrs. Caribou had made for us. When all these things were ready we sat down to eat.

It was really quiet and peaceful sitting there just alongside the river, listening to the gentle gurgle of the current while the water flowed on by, the river slowly journeying towards unknown destinations far beyond any imagination. Dad seemed to be in a melancholy state of mind and in his voice was a certain and distinct tinge of emotion we seldom heard. He spoke softly as he shared memories of times before, a small glimpse into a monument of recollections already gathered—many of which, presumably, had been triggered earlier as we passed by the old log cabin. It wasn't often that Dad shared his personal side with us. And so we listened intently, and with great interest:

> *My grandfather,* Dad told us, *Martin Benjamin Olsen, was born in Aalborg, Denmark on May 1, 1897. He was the oldest of seven children and emigrated to North America, arriving in the United States at the tender age of thirteen. It wasn't long before Martin realized it wasn't the place for him and came north to Canada, pursuing dreams of establishing great wealth through the trapping industry. There was a brief stopover at Dauphin, Manitoba before he succumbed to the temptation to keep travelling. His journey took him west into Saskatchewan, the next province over,*

where he eventually settled in and around the Big River region. Martin, along with others, helped establish the Isle a la Crosse Fish Company in Saskatchewan. In 1914, Martin met Anna Ethier and they married the same year. Sadly, their marriage was short-lived. Anna gave birth to two daughters before her tragic death in the influenza epidemic of 1918.

Their first child, Florence Dolly Mary Olsen, was born on August 31, 1915; their second daughter, Neta Myrtle Olsen, arrived a couple of years later, on April 21, 1917. After Anna's passing, Martin had various nannies look after his two girls. One of the nannies who took care of them for some time was old lady Patterson, nicknamed O-souse, *Cree for "mouse tail." O-souse was married to Dave Patterson and was a midwife in those times. She spoke only Cree and so the two girls learned to speak and understand the language fluently, although they lost much of it as time went on. Dave Patterson moved to La Ronge and today there is a local park named in his honour.*

Finally, one young lady came to look after the girls and stayed. Alice Lein was introduced into the family and Martin eventually married her in 1927 so Alice became fondly known as the "dreaded" stepmother and eventually the "mother-in-law," until her death from a massive haemorrhage in the winter of 1943.

In the late summer of 1933, Florence and a boy she had been seeing went for a boat ride. Somewhere along the shore, they stopped and he had his way with her. On August 25, 1934, my father, James Edward Olsen, was born. Florence and the boy wanted to get married, but his parents thought he was too young. So Martin hired his friend, John Diefenbaker, to represent Florence at

Florence Olsen

a support trial. Mr. Diefenbaker couldn't make it so he sent someone from his firm. Florence was awarded $6 a month in child support.

Martin Olsen raised Jim as his own son. But sometimes this is not always good, and with "stepmother" still there, Florence felt it would be better to marry and take her son with her, so when Tom Nicholson happened on the scene, he was seen as a way out.

Thomas David Nicholson was born on October 27, 1900 in Lingdale, England to William and Sarah Ann Nicholson. He came to Canada in 1926 and arrived in Big River to homestead in 1930. He held various jobs in the surrounding district, working in the mill, cooking for bush camps, firefighting, and splitting cord-wood. He was working at a farm near Martin Olsen's when he became aware of Florence. He was at least ten years older than she was but he courted her and on March 28, 1937 they were married. And then the children came. Jim's siblings are, in descending order: Priscilla Rose, William Benjamin, Alice La Verne, Florence Grace Elizabeth and Ruth Nadine. There were three stillborn as well. Florence eventually left Tom and moved out west with her youngest daughter, Nadine, ultimately arriving at her sister Myrtle's in Prince George, British Columbia. And there she stayed.[1]

1 Nadine Nicholson and Priscilla Pister. "Florence Dolly Mary Olsen - Family Gathering 1995." Community Communications. 1995.

Dad reminisced about the cabin on Selenite Point. It was here Martin had begun his dream of fame and fortune in the fur trade, but alas! it is always harder than it seems, and after a few attempts at trapping and raising fur there, Martin eventually moved on to another location at Egg Lake near La Ronge. Meanwhile, Florence continued to look after Dad for several years, until shortly into her marriage with Tom, though it was an ongoing struggle from the start of their relationship. This gradually worsened as Dad got older and Florence continued to have children with Tom. Without the support of his grandfather, Martin, the situation deteriorated rapidly and it became intolerable for Dad to live at home any longer. There was a final clash with his stepfather, Tom, which almost led to blows on Dad's part, that proved to him he could no longer call this place home. Nor was he welcome to. It was the final straw for Dad, and at the very early age of twelve he faced the open world on his own.

Years later, Grandma Florence shared with us those final moments before Dad left. The heart-wrenching pain she felt, the hopelessness. There wasn't anything she could do but let the tears flow and watch silently as her firstborn walked away and disappeared into a life obscured by uncertainty, worried about what the future held for her son.

Many years later Martin returned to the Big River area and shortly thereafter Florence received the sad news of his death. He had been walking along the shore of Stony Lake near Big River and had stopped for a rest when he was struck down by a massive heart attack and died. This was a real shock to Florence and especially Dad. Although Martin had been quite hard on him, he had still treated Dad as a son. All of this had a great impact on Florence and no doubt greatly influenced the direction of her life. Still, Florence continued her relationship with Tom even after her son's departure but shortly after the death of her dad circumstances changed and in 1964 she moved on.

Tom eventually moved into a senior citizens' home in Big River and passed on many years ago, leaving the wonderful and lasting legacy of his children and children's children.

After Dad left home, he returned to the cabin at Selenite Point; it was the only place he knew that felt like a home to him. By this time, a German man named Anton Mylengar had taken up residence there. Anton basically took over where Martin left off and took Dad in with open arms, appreciative of the company. It was to this cabin Dad came until Anton retired to a new home on the southwest side of Smoothstone, just north of the Schloegle homestead and the sand beach. His new place gave Anton road access and the freedom to travel year round, but he got a bit eccentric in his old age.

And so the cabin at Selenite Point became a stopping place to hang your hat for a season, Dad told us. Others used the place, too, even if it was just for a short period of time. Frank Schloegle used the old cabin for his mink ranch and George Olson stayed there too.

But now the day was wearing on and Dad, having realized the time, abruptly stopped and quickly gathered his thoughts of the past and moved us back into to the present.

Knowing it would take several hours to cross the portage with our supplies we didn't delay any longer. Now with everything in order and Mum and Dad each with a pack sack and a travois to haul, it was time to go, so with our minds set and looking forward to the other end, we were off.

mahigan portage

It was almost noon when we entered the portage. The fresh autumn air was still quite cool even though the sun was well up by this time. It was pleasant to see how the sunlight penetrated the thick forest of tall evergreens, giving light to an otherwise dark and damp part of the overland trail. The ground in this area was covered over in a thick layer of green moss, and a similar type called old man's beard hung down off the branches like sheets of light green tinsel. This part of the portage was spooky, but on parts of the trail where the deciduous trees were it was bright and vibrant, especially where the leaves hadn't fallen. It was there the sunlight caused an explosion of colour, shading each leaf in a different hue of autumn glory, and it made you feel warm and alive with excitement.

The portage was well kept and remained cleared. During the winter months, Mr. Schloegle would pull a large sleigh through with a team of horses while commercial fishing Big Mahigan. He would come in after freeze-up and bring us extra goods and news from the outside world.

Mahigan portage and an abundance of thick moss

While walking along the trail, we had the wonderful pleasure of hearing the cheerful singing of birds, so loud it seemed they were trying to make up for the ones that had already left on their migratory flight south for warmer regions. Whatever the reason for the chorus of song, it was a joy to listen to.

After walking for some time, the trail gradually rose to the crest of a small knoll and it was here the portage returned to the river. The bank had a steep decline that dropped rather quickly to the water's edge. The area above this bend in the river was level and flat, and tall grass lined the bank. This was a great vantage point—you could see both ways along the river—and it made for a very picturesque view.

At this time of year, the river runs a lot slower and is at its shallowest, averaging about two feet in depth and ten feet in width. During high water and heavy spring run-off, the river runs quite swiftly and increases in width up to thirty feet or more, with many sections becoming rapids along the way.

This spot was a great place to have lunch and a bit of a rest, shaded by a large stand of Jack pine but free from underbrush, giving it a park-like atmosphere. The ground was sandy, covered over with caribou moss and low bush cranberries. There were a few blueberries as well, although they were scattered about and small in size due to the old forest. Blueberries thrive a year or two after an area burns. Once a forest fire has swept through, it opens up the area for new growth. But even without the blueberries, there were a lot of cranberries here and since it was a bush favourite, Mum picked enough to fill a tin bucket. Later she'd turn the cranberries into a sweet sauce that went very well with fresh bannock. For us, the sweeter the better!

This particular spot in the portage had been a rest area for many others over the years, yet the only evidence that remained was a circle of stones that outlined the firepit and a few remnants of black charcoal from the last fire. "So many people and yet so untouched," were Dad's words, encompassing the honour of true bush people and their respect for nature and the environment, men and women of times past and present. Now it was our turn.

Dad ambled down to the river and filled two pails with water—one for making tea and the other to pour on the fire when we finished lunch. Mum, Clarence and I went about gathering dry sticks and pieces of wood for the campfire. It wasn't long before we had a hot fire on the go. A small pole held the pail just above the flames until the water was boiling, ready for tea. Mum put sandwiches made from thinly sliced roast moose alongside the hot coals to heat up before we ate. Afterwards, our bellies full, there was only one important matter that needed attention: an afternoon nap! And under these circumstances we succumbed to the warm afternoon sun.

We woke to coolness in the air. The sun had gone behind a small cloud and when the shadow spread over our spot there was a noticeable chill that acted as our alarm clock. We got up and made ourselves ready for the last leg of the journey. The small fire had burnt itself out, yet to ensure it was completely extinguished, Dad poured the remains of the tea and water into the ashes then stirred the wet mass to ensure any live coals were completely doused. With the fire secured we got under way.

We had only been walking for a few minutes when Dad came to a full stop. He pointed ahead along the portage and there, standing on the trail, was a large bull moose looking at us! The bull was breathing heavy and its great chest heaved with loud whistling noises as it gasped. Dad slowly lowered his travois (he was carrying the motor) and removed the rifle from across his shoulders to be ready should the animal attack. A moose is a very large animal and they stand extremely tall on dry ground. With its raspy gasps for air and huge frame we were acutely aware of being very small creatures in comparison. The bull's massive frame seemed larger than life and very intimidating in those close quarters; its huge set of antlers took up the width of the portage. There was nowhere to go. The situation was immediately intense.

We didn't have to wait long before finding out why the moose was there. Up until then it had been quiet and the only sound had come from the moose—but suddenly timber wolves crossed the portage in all directions! The wolves detected our scent and immediately faded back into the forest, only to form a circle around us just beyond eyesight. Then they began to howl.

By now, Mum had gathered us to her and we took refuge against one of the larger trees at the side of the portage. But

Dad had had enough and, shouldering his rifle, he waited for a wolf to cross the trail. He didn't have long to wait. One of the larger wolves appeared at a dead run and, though only visible for a split second, Dad was ready. He fired off a round, killing the wolf despite its speed. It was a large male with a thin coat of greyish-white summer hair and there were a number of spots on the animal that were quite rubbed, making the pelt worthless—although that was the least of our worries at the moment.

As a rule, wolves usually try to avoid larger animals because the chances of getting hurt or even killed are considerable. But contrary to this rule, their willingness to attack depends on a number of things. For instance, if the wolves corner a large animal, they will stay close and worry it to keep it from feeding until it becomes exhausted and weak. The same goes in a chase; they will keep their prey moving and take turns attacking from behind. And the most motivating factor is how hungry they are. Mature adult wolves gorge when the occasion arises, and in a land of plenty like this they only get serious in a major attack if they haven't eaten in seven to ten days. Now and then there might be one renegade that goes on a killing spree. What causes this is uncertain and has been open to speculation around many an evening campfire. For whatever reason, once a hunt is started there is very little that will change the wolf's course of action. In general, wolves will avoid humans at all costs and rarely do people have encounters or even see them due to their uncanny ability—a sixth sense—of knowing what is around them. But if you do come across them there's generally a reasonable explanation: sometimes it's mere accident, and sometimes you've encroached on their territory during mating season or when they're heavy into a hunt, as our experience suggested.

A trapper once told us this story about a wolf's sixth sense:

A trapper once found a young wolf cub left on its own. The reason for its apparent abandonment was unknown, but could have been any one of a number of things—life in the wilderness is not an easy one.

The trapper captured the cub and raised it alongside his sled dogs. His cabin was located in the furthest reaches of a bay, facing the main body of water. Half a mile out and to the right was a point of land that kept the rest of the lake hidden from view.

When it was early spring and very nice out, the trapper decided to sit outside and soak in a little warmth from the afternoon sun. All the sled dogs were spread across the ground sound asleep, including the young wolf. The trapper sat, admiring the scenery, watching the natural phenomenon of rising air currents caused by warm air above the cold, white ice. The dancing mirages created a mesmerizing spectacle.

Suddenly the young wolf raised its head, cocked both ears and looked intently across the lake in the direction of the point. The dogs showed no sign of waking whatsoever, but the wolf kept its gaze riveted to the distant jut of land and let out a soft whimper just before the figure of a man came into view. The trapper remained silent, monitoring the difference between the wolf and his dogs. Eventually the curious dogs woke to see what the wolf pup was whimpering about and when they spotted the man they arose in a frenzied uproar! [2]

2 This story was passed down by the late John Fietz, a bushman and friend who trapped north of La Ronge. In 2008, a man was killed by wolves in Northern Saskatchewan.

Luckily for us, the wolves went one way and the moose went another, heading for the river and safety. Dad's intervention had ensured our safe passage and allowed the moose to live another day. We were all a little shook up, but no worse for wear and so, with a lasting memory, again we set out.

It was late afternoon when we came down the hill near the end of the portage and the shore of Little Mahigan. The lake was quite shallow and narrow at this end and the slight breeze had completely died down, leaving nature to fill in the void.

There is always a sense of anticipation when arriving at a lake as to what you might see. There was a lot of racket on the water—ducks making a fuss as they fed—but there were no large animals we could see. And after a brief look we did not delay, for we still had a mile to go and it was close to nightfall. Once the outboard was mounted on the small boat and our gear stowed inside, all of us got in and headed up the shore to the cabin. As we came around the last corner the first thing we noticed in the dimming light was that our small shack-tent had been damaged; there were huge, gaping holes in the roof of the tent. A bear had paid our place a visit while we were gone and Dad said a few choice words—things I certainly won't repeat here!

We were fortunate, though—the damage inside was minimal, mostly due to the fact that the supplies we'd had in the shack-tent had already been transferred over to the new cabin before we'd left for Big River. The clean-up was just another item to add to the long list of things to do and repair, but the shack-tent would have to wait for another day; this one was coming to an end and we were all bone-tired.

Dad lit the gas lantern and built a fire in the drum stove while Mum took out the bed rolls and made up the beds. Once things were unpacked and temporarily set aside for the night, we had a bowl of soup and bannock. Dad shared his disappointment at having to kill the wolf but still felt it had been necessary for our safety and we were thankful for that.

It was time to call it a day.

a typical fall day

Daylight arrived, and with it a strong north wind that blew down the length of the lake, creating rough, mean-looking waves. The heavy gusts churned the water into whitecaps that chased each other down the lake in a zigzag game of tag. With this spectacle before us, there was good reason to be thankful we had come across the big water of Smoothstone Lake the day before. Fall had arrived with a vengeance and with the wind came a real chill that felt like it blew right through you.

It was just as well that the day came in the way it did as we were very sore and tired from freighting our gear across the overland trail. There were no immediate plans for travelling any further, at least not for a day or so anyway. Even though we'd left our camp in order before heading out, there always seemed to be a multitude of tasks waiting for us when we returned. It was like nature made a list of things to do during our absence, things that were either forgotten or things that had been put on hold. Amazing how these items could become a priority and how fast things changed, even in a few days!

Little Mahigan Lake, looking east from our cabin

One thing Dad taught Clarence and me at a very early age was to leave the cabin ready for our return; things like having the wood box filled, the block wood split lengthwise to make kindling, and shavings and birchbark to make a quick fire. Matches and candles were stored in a rodent-proof container to keep them dry and safe. These things were not only a convenience but a matter of survival and needed to be readily available, especially if it was late and dark when you got back. Chances were that you'd be cold, tired and possibly wet.

Man, the to-do list was extensive! There was grass to cut—it seemed like it had grown up as high as the bottom sill of the windows. The water barrel needed filling (it had been drained to prevent it from freezing, expanding and bursting the barrel while we were gone, and besides, it needed to be filled with fresh water as it would have gone quite stale in our absence). The items we carried over had to be put away in their proper place, and, of course, there was the damage the bear had caused.

After making a general survey of the shack-tent and assessing the worst of it, we tackled the clean-up. There's one thing about bears and tents that seem to go hand in hand: when they enter a place you just know there'll be another hole someplace because they never leave the same way they come in. Bears make a real mess of a canvas tent and it's possible they like the sound of the canvas as it tears. Another strange thing is that bears love the smell of gas cans, hoses or any other container for that matter. They chew and puncture them with their teeth. Given enough time, a bear will wreak havoc on everything in and around your camp. It's extremely important the cabin and area is left tidy and any containers that might entice the animal be properly stored to prevent damage.

After we took the tent from its frame, Mum took up a needle and started patching the tears with the extra canvas we had in our supplies. The rip was stitched up first and then a patch was cut large enough to cover the tear by several inches and marked. Canvas adhesive was applied just short of the mark to allow the patch to be hemmed before stitching.

Meanwhile, Dad cleaned the debris out of the small shack and repaired the broken rafters and shelves. Once the tent was repaired, it was set back over the rafters and pulled down tight along the perimeter of the walls. Plywood nailing strips were used to hold it in place. For additional weather-proofing, a waterproof tarpaulin went over the shack-tent to add extra protection and ensure the interior remained dry. As winter approached and the trapping season began, this little shack-tent would be the place we'd prepare our furs.

It had taken most of the day to get the shack-tent repaired and ready for service. Now with evening fast approaching,

Mum started preparing the evening meal. Tonight the main course would be small game, which was yet to be announced, fresh potatoes and bannock. Also, Mum was going to boil some of the cranberries she'd picked earlier and make jam sauce for dessert. Meanwhile, Dad gathered up his rifle. With the single shot .22- calibre rimfire tucked under his arm, he was off to get meat for our evening meal.

Even with a clear sky, dusk approached rapidly when the sun went behind the hill at the back of the cabin. Today it was even more noticeable due to the heavy cloud cover. The wind never let up at all and on more than one occasion we raised concerns about the tall Jack pine trees around the cabin, hoping they wouldn't blow over, although Mum assured us they were healthy and strong and would be okay. As for us boys, we had other thoughts. Therefore, it was important that we get our regular chores done before dark. The afternoon was chilly and we needed an extra layer to keep out the cold, but after moving around it wasn't so bad and with some effort we managed to fill both water barrel and wood box.

The fire in our barrel stove radiated waves of heat that felt great after coming in from the damp fall air outside. We could smell the coffee that seemed to be constantly brewing on top of the stove. Now that the chores were done Clarence and I stood around the stove, soaking up the heat and watching Mum prepare food. She mixed up the ingredients for the bannock: flour, salt and baking powder. To this dry mixture she kneaded in lard and then stirred in enough water to form a ball. This was placed on a floured tin and the dough kneaded to form a flat oval. She used the tines of a fork to make small indentations that would allow the dough to cook through. Finally, the bannock was placed in the small tin cookstove to bake and soon the aroma of fresh bannock wafted through the air.

Mum's kitchen

Mum then put about two cups of cranberries in a small pot and added just enough water to cover them. The berries were set on the stove to boil before she stirred in a half cup of sugar. After the sugar was added, the berries were allowed to simmer for a short spell before being poured into a glass jar to cool. This was more like a sauce than a jam or jelly; for us boys, though, it could've used a lot more sugar because it still had a bite to it! However, our complaints had no effect whatsoever. The reality was that it was sweet enough already and made a great spread for our bannock.

Dad returned with three spruce grouse for the evening meal. He'd cleaned them out in the bush and they were ready to be cooked. The meat went straight into a pot of boiling water and was finished about the same time the bannock came out of the oven. It amazes me that Mum and Dad were able to coordinate meals in this way but we didn't think anything of it then.

We washed up in the basin by the door while the table was set with the bare minimum of utensils. A plate, cup, butter knife, spoon and fork each. We all had different styles of cutlery, but it didn't matter as these were more than adequate and they served their purpose.

The meat from the birds was taken out of the pot and trimmed into thin slices, there were mashed potatoes and hot bannock, and you couldn't ask for anything more. Dessert was fresh-sliced bannock dipped in hot cranberry syrup—Mum must've added a bit more sugar so maybe our whining paid off.

While we polished off our dessert, the last bit of light on the eastern shore melted away into darkness. Dad lit the gas lantern and when the mantle came to a full glow, the one-room cabin was bathed in light.

My brother and I got tucked into bed and like all good boys we went directly to sleep—right! We listened as Mum and Dad went over the day's events and then their plans for the following days prior to freeze-up. Their conversation turned to the supply of meat we needed for the winter, but with no freezer, filling this necessity would be put off until the weather turned cold enough to keep the meat from spoiling. We also learned another trapper would be sharing part of our trapline and Dad was expecting him to show up soon. We weren't sure where he would build his cabin, but speculated that it would be further south along the lake.

There was a considerable amount of discussion concerning the bear that had been through camp, and since it had been here once, it was pretty much a certainty that it would come again. This time of year they stayed close to their dens and only made short foraging trips for food before retiring for the winter, so Dad suspected both the bear and its den weren't far away and there was a good chance the bear would show up again real soon.

Somewhere amid the soft conversation, the warmth of the cabin and the steady hiss from the gas lantern, it was lights out.

a neighbour

It seemed like we'd just closed our eyes for only a moment and then we were being awakened. Dad told us to be quiet but to get up and look outside. We made our way over to the window to see what all the excitement was about.

A cow moose was wading parallel to the shoreline, up to her belly in water about twenty feet out, feeding while she moved along. She moved her head from side to side, searching out the weeds ahead while her long ears turned constantly, tuned for any sound of danger. The moose came to an abrupt stop when it caught scent of our cabin and its inhabitants. Her long head swung around and she looked directly at us, the large, round nose and big eyes clearly visible in the early morning dawn. Even though daylight was just approaching, it was still quite dark out, but there was no mistaking the intent of her gaze. The moose stood absolutely motionless in the water, staring at the cabin for what seemed like several minutes before finally making a move.

We held our breath as we waited for her to decide what she was looking at and what she should do about this strange structure in the forest. If she did see us in the darkened cabin, I'm sure we made an odd sight for sure, especially with our round faces pressed flat against the surface of the glass as we peered out. And once she moved, apparently having determined that we were beneath her further notice, we all exhaled at the same moment, a little breathless from the experience.

Although it was early and dawn was only on the horizon, after the morning's entertainment there wasn't much use in going back to bed. The coal oil lamp was lit and the fire in the stove rekindled. The coffee pot was placed on the camp stove to percolate and our day was under way. Soon the cabin was warm and the aroma of fresh coffee filled the small cabin. Mum stirred up orange juice drink mix and set the table. Meanwhile, Dad whipped up his famous pancakes. As breakfast took place, the sun rose over the far hills to light up the eastern skyline in a blaze of pink and orange.

The lake was calm and it was cool outside with a few fog patches spread out across the lake. Once the heat from the rising sun warmed the area, the fog began to lift like columns of smoke swirling skywards until they disappeared. The thin layer of white fog floating just above the water followed and soon the lake was clear. The rising air currents started a ripple on the surface of the lake and a gentle breeze began to blow. The fall ducks started up a racket, splashing up a storm during their morning bath, preparing themselves for the day.

After breakfast was out of the way, chores began. And the first thing on the list today was to get all the weeds and grass cut, especially around the cabin as the long grass attracted mice and bugs. Mice and squirrels are a real nuisance in a trapper's cabin; they chew on everything, leaving holes and spoiling food, spreading their droppings all over the place. It's very important to keep your staples stored in a secure location for health reasons.

The scrub board, Mum's knuckle-buster!

We were desperately short of fresh meat so Dad wanted to go see what he could find; he also wanted to scout the area for fur-bearing animals and see if there was any bear sign about. With this task in mind he was off, saying he'd be back later in the day. After Dad left, Mum put a water pail on the stove to heat up for laundry. The clothes were soaked in a galvanised metal washtub and cleaned by hand using a scrubbing board. The flat, thin board was made out of a wood frame that supported a thick, ribbed glass plate. This was set into the washtub and the clothes were scrubbed against it. Mum did the laundry outside since it was still nice enough to do so, but it wouldn't be too long before all this would have to be done indoors. It was our job to keep the water running by keeping the water barrel and water pail full. Mum used a large bar of hand soap for laundry detergent; it lasted longer and was less bulky for transportation.

After the clothes were run through the wash, Mum took them down to the lake to rinse the soap out of them, leaning over the edge of the short dock projecting out from the small sand beach. The majority of the clothes were then hung from the clothesline to dry. The clothesline was attached to a corner of the cabin and the other end to one of the many large Jack pine trees that surrounded it. The rest of the washing that would be needed right away was taken inside and hung on a small clothes hanger off the back wall of the cabin near the stove.

Mum had always liked puzzles and now that she had a bit of free time she started one on a piece of cardboard cut to fit the final picture. It was playtime for us boys too, and the hill behind the cabin was a great playground. Even though climbing back and forth required a lot of energy, we had a blast rolling down the hill. Mind you, that didn't help the clean clothes' situation, but it did get us out of Mum's hair for awhile.

Dad arrived back at midday with a lot of news and a packsack full of fresh venison from a young buck he'd come across. He'd trimmed the meat off the bone so was able to bring it all back in one trip. The larger pieces were hung on meat hooks fastened to a pole tied across two trees a short distance from the cabin. The smaller pieces he set on wire mesh supported above a firepit by a small pole structure in the form of a tipi. That was where the meat and fish were smoked, dried and cooked. In short order we had a fire going to start drying the meat. The smaller leftovers went straight into the stewing pot to simmer and slow cook. Dad wasn't particularly fond of deer meat, so he'd also bagged several rabbits. One of his favourite dishes was made by placing the rabbit meat in a Dutch oven—a large cast-iron pot with a heavy lid—which in turn was put over the fire and allowing the meat to slow cook in its own gravy. We'd have both the venison stew and simmered rabbit for our evening meal.

Meanwhile, it was back to the never-ending chores. There was still the hundred-yard gill net to sort out. It needed to be cleaned and a few waterlogged floats replaced. A large northern pike, also known as jackfish, had torn the mesh and it was in bad need of repair. The net was stored in a wood fish box and to clean and untangle the mesh webbing Dad removed the net a little at a time and spread it across a tarpaulin with leads on one side and floats on the other—as it was pulled across the tarpaulin, the weeds and anything that had been collected while it was in the water were tugged out, waterlogged floats were replaced with new ones and all the tears were sewn shut. Once this procedure had been accomplished over the entire length of the net, it was pulled evenly back into the tub with lead and float together and the mesh looped into piles so as not to get tangled. Now it was ready for future use.

Dad told us that earlier in the day he'd come out on a small round meadow when he'd heard noise further south. The faint sound came from the direction of the portage into Mahigan and it sounded man-made. There was a good chance that someone had come across the portage and since we'd been expecting a new neighbour that was more than likely who it was. Dad asked us to tag along and boat down to see if he'd arrived.

Without any hesitation we were at the water's edge and in the boat. Dad started the outboard and we motored down the lake, the shoreline whizzing by. We chased a few ducks; some took off in flight, others remained on the water, eventually diving beneath the surface to try and escape the approaching craft and the ominous sound of the motor in the stillness.

It was a short journey by boat and soon we came around the last bend at the south end of the lake. At this point we could see someone standing along the shoreline, waving. We could barely make him out as the tall grass and long-standing bulrushes against the towering spruce trees almost engulfed him. Dad slowed the motor down and we were soon near enough to

Our wood boat and motor

see that it was indeed our new neighbour, George Olson. He had come down to wait by the water's edge after hearing the sound of our outboard motor.

George Olson was a short, stout Norwegian from Oslo, Norway who had immigrated to Canada as a very young man and eventually found his way to Big River. George had come over with his dad and older brother, Olif, after being enticed by the news of great wealth and opportunities the Canadian prairies offered. Their destination was Saskatchewan.

They arrived by train and the end of the line for them happened to be Shellbrook, Saskatchewan. They arrived in the dead of winter and to their shock it was forty below zero! So much for the propaganda pictures of warm sunny skies and fields of green!

Now here they were without work. They stayed in Shellbrook for a short time at a boarding house, doing odd jobs until that spring when his brother was hired for a full-time job near Christopher Lake. George was then taken in by George and Abigail Charles to help them as a farmhand. George Charles was a First Nations Indian man residing at Sturgeon Lake. Sturgeon Lake is an Indian reservation not far from Shellbrook near the city of Prince Albert, Saskatchewan.

George Olson the Norwegian

It was at this time George and Olif's dad decided to return to Oslo, a decision not taken lightly as chances were he'd never see his boys again. This indeed became the case as time progressed. But there was some comfort in the fact that their dad had left only after knowing both boys were in good hands.

George stayed with this First Nations Indian family until he was able to go out on his own the following year. George acknowledged that he would have stayed on longer—they'd accepted him fully, but it was tough living at the time, and even though they were raising their own cattle, it was illegal for the Charles family not only to sell their beef, but to keep any for themselves. It was a difficult time for the Charles family and even though George was grateful for their hospitality, he chose to leave the following

Joan Mirasty (my future wife), Abigail Charles, Donald Mirasty and George Charles

spring to ease their burden. He then made his way to Big River.

Once George arrived at Big River, he did some freighting north to the communities of Beauval and Buffalo Narrows, and for a short time ran the mail from Big River to communities north by dog team until a permanent road was in place. And like many others of this era, George tried his hand at logging, commercial fishing and working as a farmhand. George had been jilted by a young lady he was fond of and from that time onward chose to remain a bachelor, becoming very set in his ways. To this end, he found himself challenged by the solitude of bush life as a trapper, and so, between jobs, he'd decided to spend a season trapping.

George had already known Dad for a number of years and, in fact, Dad had stayed with him—George being one of the transient trappers who hung his beaver hat at the cabin on Selenite Point. And that was the start of a lifelong friendship. Oh, to be sure there were ups and downs, but when it came down to the crunch, the friendship always came out on top. And such was the case for both Clarence and me as well. Unbeknownst to me at this time, the descendants of Magnus and William Twatt, George Charles and that friendship with George Olson were to become very important in my life many years later.

Originally, Sturgeon Lake First Nation was named the "William Twatt Band" after a Scotsman who was directly involved with the signing of Treaty Six in 1876. His father, Magnus Twatt, had sailed over from Orkney, Scotland after being recruited to the Hudson Bay Company. Shortly after Magnus arrived he met a Cree Indian woman from Cumberland House, Saskatchewan and they had two sons, Mansack and Willock, and a daughter, Betsy. Magnus worked as a joiner and canoe maker, and helped build Fort Carlton, east of Prince Albert. He made several trips back home to Orkney before his untimely death at Carrot River, Saskatchewan in 1801.

William stayed on and established the reservation known as Sturgeon Lake First Nation today—incidentally the First Nation that John Diefenbaker became an honorary band chief of, even wearing the complete headdress. Even though he was prime minister of Canada at the time, this little reserve tagged him with a new nickname: "Dief the Chief," being a local and all from Prince Albert, Saskatchewan. This name soon became known nationwide and was used during and after Diefenbaker's term in office.[2]

As the small boat landed, there were smiles all around. It was good to see George and he was overjoyed to see that we had made it also. We were each glad to have a neighbour through the long winter months. George invited us up to where he had pitched a ten by twelve canvas prospector's tent. We sat on the blocks of wood he used for the fire. George offered Dad a cup of coffee and orange juice for us boys. The coffee was piping hot already as it had been sitting on the small tin airtight stove George

2 Kim Twatt, Orkney, Scotland. http://www.orcadian.co.uk/features/articles/kimtwatt.htm. Accessed Feb. 11, 2011

used for everything: heating, cooking and drying. The juice was made from dry crystals added to fresh lake water. While George was attending to the beverages, he brought us up to date with his current news.

The area he'd chosen for his small cabin was almost at the south end of the lake on the west bank, past the portage by several hundred yards and close to where the creek began its journey to Smoothstone Lake. It was a lower, flatter part of the region, well-sheltered from the wind in all directions, and heavily wooded with spruce trees and thick green moss. About a hundred feet from the shoreline, George had cleared out a space large enough to build his cabin. It was a very convenient location since all the building materials were on site and readily available.

The only issue with building in a low and sheltered area is that it can get quite damp during the summer and fall, and the cabin itself would decay in a few years. But George wasn't bothered by that—his cabin was only to be a temporary structure and would be sufficient for his needs. We visited for awhile, then it was time to get back home. Dad said he would stop in and help George with the build over the next few days. It would be a small trapper's cabin so wouldn't take very long to construct. With that we said our goodbyes and left for home.

Halfway up the lake we could smell the aroma of the waiting stew waiting. We did, however, stop once on the way home to pick up some fresh water from the spring that ran down from the hills on the east side of the lake, even though it was all right to drink the lake water itself. We parked the boat and filled the water jugs just where the spring started to flow into the lake and the water is clear, cold and perfect for drinking. These jugs would last us a few days.

Over the next several days, George's small cabin was completed and his residence set up for the winter. Only twelve by twelve and seven feet high, it was very cosy but would be easy to keep warm. The wall logs were chinked inside and out with the heavy moss found around the cabin, and the roof was made of small logs packed tightly together with a polyethylene cover and a thick layer of moss for insulation. There was one door and a small window for light. The door was made out of slabs cut from a log and the hinge was a piece of rolled up canvas, cut the full length of the door and fastened on with small nails. A looped rope held it firmly in place when George wanted to keep the door closed. Leftover plastic wrapped around a sawn plank frame and fitted into an opening in the logs became a window. You couldn't see much through it, but it did let the light in.

And now came the waiting. When would freeze-up come?

freeze-up!

Over the next few days the temperature dropped steadily, especially at night when we really noticed the chill. The last of the autumn leaves were gone now and most of the ducks had disappeared—except for a hardy few intent on braving it out to the very last. Our fall chores were mostly done; we'd hauled in a good stockpile of cord wood from around the area, and sawed and split a good quantity of block wood. Our cabin was well-insulated, warm and comfortable.

And then one morning we woke up to a very distinct quietness that filled the air. There was an immediate reaction to this stillness. Instantly curious and excited, we jumped out of bed and raced over to the windows for a look. And there! The lake was covered over in a smooth, black sheet of ice that stretched from shore to shore.

We all spoke at once: "Freeze up!"

We quickly slipped into our clothes and went down to the small dock for a firsthand look at this wonder of nature. It felt warmer out—the ice and frost had sealed in the moisture and made the air drier. Dad went to the shack-tent for the steel ice chisel and proceeded to test the thickness of the ice. It needed to be at least two inches thick before we could walk on it, and there was a good chance it already was since the temperature had really dropped the day before and it had been a bitterly cold night. Even before nightfall we'd seen the surface of the lake looking thick and dark, and the water slushy.

The ice chisel test was proof positive that overnight the temperature had really plummeted. The lake froze surprisingly well; there was just enough ice to safely walk on, at least along the shoreline anyway. With this bit of knowledge and growing excitement we hurried back into the warm cabin. Now that the lake had enough ice to walk on, it was time to start setting runs on the trapline. After a great breakfast of bacon, eggs and sliced bannock, Dad was chomping at the bit to get started. He gathered his overcoat and packsack, filled earlier with all the necessary equipment for the trail.

He used a sleigh to haul the rest of the gear. The sleigh had two runners with cross braces at short intervals along their length and to this a piece of rope had been added for pulling the sleigh. It wasn't fancy, but it saved the back. Dad took both rifles, his .22 rimfire, a bolt action single-shot Cooey and the .303 British Enfield bolt action. They were placed in the sleigh alongside the packsack ready for travel, and with a tug on the rope he was gone.

For safety, Dad travelled only a short distance from the shoreline; sometimes the ice doesn't freeze to the same thickness further out. This happens on larger lakes and depends on the currents beneath. As he pulled the sleigh along, he tested the ice at regular intervals by swinging an axe and delivering a blow to the ice; he knew just how thick it was by this long-practised method.

It's always a bit difficult to walk on fresh black ice—it can be tricky to do without slipping. Eventually you get into the swing of it, though, you start by holding your legs stiff and getting a shuffle going, and as soon as you catch on you can make good progress. By midday Dad had been around Little Mahigan and through the small portage at the northeast end of the lake and out onto Big Mahigan.

The short portage ran parallel to the small river connecting these two lakes. Because of the current, this small river would stay open for quite awhile, and it was a good place for river otter, mink and other animals travelling along its banks. The big lake had just as much ice on it so Dad carried on further up the west shore to where beavers had built a big lodge. It was tucked in behind a small point of land on the north shore. There were a few lodges scattered about between the lakes and this was one of several he'd seen today, the first being on Little Mahigan not far from our cabin.

Dad still had a short distance to go before rounding the small point near the beaver lodge, but he never got there. At that moment, a bull moose jumped to its feet. It had bedded down for the afternoon in a thick growth of shoreline bulrushes. As the moose charged for the bank, Dad pulled up the sleigh and grabbed the rifle. In one smooth motion he drew back the bolt action and jacked a shell into the chamber, then swung around, bringing the rifle to his shoulder and simultaneously sighting in just as the moose scrambled over the bank. Just as it disappeared into the underbrush, eye, sight, target and trigger finger connected and with a loud *BANG!* the rifle jolted backwards, kicking back powerfully as the exploding gunpowder pushed the deadly projectile out at an incredible speed. Then all was silent—except for the sound of the rifle shot echoing off into the distance until even that was no more.

Winter's moose meat

There was no need to hurry now. Dad sat down on the sleigh and rolled a cigarette, taking about ten minutes to just listen, but there was no other sound. He picked up the rifle and walked over to where the moose had gone in over the bank. He followed the trail a short distance in and found the animal. A clean shot through the lung had killed it. Dad took a closer look. It was a two-year-old bull, perfect for our winter's meat supply.

Dad backtracked out to the lake to get the sleigh and packsack; he needed the axe to clear a trail into the kill site. Once it was cleared, he attended to the moose. First, all the insides were taken out and the choice parts set aside to be taken home for a feast, then he cut it into quarters. The sleigh would only hold a little, so Dad loaded just one of the hind quarters. Even so it had to be strapped down. The rest of the meat he placed on clean grass, covered over with the hide and some spruce boughs to keep it hidden from ravens.

It was quite a work-out and he took a break to make tea and have a bit of lunch. Near the waterline where summer's waves had exposed the sand a fire was quickly made with dry reeds and small bush found nearby. Out of the packsack came the teapot, and with the axe Dad chopped a hole through the ice for water. Soon the kettle was boiling and Dad tossed a couple of teabags in just before taking it off the fire to steep. Small pieces of moose meat threaded on sticks sizzled over the fire. A hot cup of tea and a bit of moose meat for nourishment gave Dad energy for the trip home.

After making sure the fire was out, he got underway. The ice was smooth and clear and the sleigh glided along freely, even under the weight of the load it carried. It's really neat to walk on the ice when it's clear and fresh; you can see everything under the surface—fish and underwater bugs darting here and there—and it's like walking on water. The weeds below the ice stand still without wave action to move them, a peaceful solitude frozen in time.

It wasn't long before he was back at the small portage into Little Mahigan. Because there was no snow it would be too difficult to drag everything over in one trip, so the load was split into two. It was a short hop over and soon he was underway again. From the north end of the smaller lake he could look down and see the cabin on the far shore, the smoke rising from the chimney renewing his desire to get home. With a jerk on the rope to get the load sliding and a revived shuffling gait—or as some would call it, a clear-ice jig—he set off on the final leg home. Nightfall was close when Dad pulled in his sleighload of meat. By the time the moose meat was carried and hung up on the meat pole, it was dark out.

It had been long day all around for both Mum and Dad. While Dad was out on the trapline, Mum had been busy with all the household chores and she'd started work on leather moccasins for us boys. We placed our feet on a section of soft moose-

My handmade wraparound moccasins

hide and then traced their outline. From this pattern the moccasin was made. To each she added a leather top with long flaps which wrapped around the ankle and tied with attached leather bindings to keep them in place. Mum would make these wraparounds over the next few days—in plenty of time before they were really needed.

Mum must have sensed our good fortune before Dad even brought in the winter's meat supply because she chose to bake bread that day. And so, after the rising and punching of the dough, adding wood to the stove, scrubbing a tubload of clothes, setting into place a piece of puzzle that had just caught her eye and finally putting the loaves of bread in the tin oven, the day came to a close. One of the last things she cooked before sitting down to eat was something we loved. Mum had saved some of the bread dough to fry into dough-gotts, sort of a fry bread, also called *lug-a-luk* by some. Moose tenderloin, mashed potato, gravy and dough-gotts were the perfect way to end a great day!

Mom made her bread dough from scratch using the most

basic of methods under the circumstances. We were fortunate enough to have the new, fast-rising yeast that was out on the market rather than the square, block yeast. This helped a great deal since the bread could be made in a few hours.

MUM'S BREAD

I cup milk (powdered)
3 tbsp sugar
2 tsp salt
4 tbsp butter (or shortening on hand)
I cup warm water
I pkg dry yeast
5+ cups flour (sifted)

Scald milk and add the salt, sugar and shortening. In a large bowl add yeast to warm water and stir in milk. Add the flour. Mix well and then knead until smooth and form into a ball, covering it with a cloth to let rise to twice its size. Make two loaves and set in a greased baking pan. Let stand for an hour then bake for half an hour at around 400 degrees. Remove when done and invert loaves to cool.

when the ice sings

It was a slow start the next morning for we had taken the liberty of sleeping in. Dad was feeling the aches and pains from the strenuous activities of the day before; it hurt to move and he was sore from head to toe. But, eventually, nature called and prompted us to get going. Dad and Mum were up first. Dad stoked the embers and soon had a roaring fire on the go, while Mum started the morning's meal using the camp stove. The camp stove had two burners. She put the kettle for making coffee on one and on the other a pot for hot cereal. A camp stove burns hot and it wasn't long before both were at a full, rolling boil.

As the heat radiated out from the stove the cabin warmed quickly; combined with the aroma of breakfast wafting through the air there was no further need to convince us to get up and soon this temptation enticed two hungry boys out from the depths of warm quilts. The table was set against the wall facing the windows and it had been built like half a picnic table; this way you could sit facing the lake. A morning ritual was to grab the binoculars and see if there was anything moving about the lake.

A lake view from the table

During open water there is always some sort of activity taking place, anything from wildlife to waterfowl. And once the water freezes over it gets a lot quieter—the waterfowl disappear for the winter months and stillness settles in. But there was still the odd morning we'd see wildlife making their way along the shoreline. Not today, though—there wasn't much of anything moving, including the wind. The temperature remained cold and well below freezing, but without the wind chill in the air it felt considerably warmer.

It was overcast with a greyish-looking sky, but it didn't look threatening—the cloud cover was relatively high and thin and there was good visibility; it might even clear up. Today we'd go and get the rest of the meat and bring it home. Dad also planned to set out a good number of squirrel snares along the way. There were some large dens scattered about the portage. The snares were made from a roll of thin copper wire, more commonly called rabbit wire.

Even with our late start we managed to be on the trail before noon. Once we arrived at the northeast end of the lake, Dad took the snares out of his packsack. The snares had been prepared in advance to save time and effort on the trail. When we came across a squirrel den, Dad would attach several of these snares to a long, narrow pole and then set the pole at an angle from the den to a nearby tree. This would act as a run and he put several of these at each location, depending on the size of the den. The red squirrel population in this part of the country is tremendous, and they thrive in the thick boreal forest that inhabits this region. The dens were plentiful then, too, and there were several families living in each one of these colonies.

It was early afternoon when we cleared the portage and made our way onto the ice. This section of the lake is quite shallow, approximately ten feet deep, and with freezing temperatures throughout the night the lake continued to form good, solid ice. We were therefore able to walk directly across the large bay rather than follow along the west shore as Dad had done previously. This saved us a considerable amount of time.

When we arrived at our destination it was time for a break. We made a fire over charcoal from the last fire and then it was time for tea and a bit of lunch of bannock and dry meat.

After a brief survey of the area, Dad informed us there was no sign of any animals that might have damaged the moose meat and the meat itself remained untouched. Since it was close to the shore, it didn't take long to bring the last of the meat out and onto the sleigh. We all did our part hauling the meat. Gunnysacks and snowshoe harnesses were used to make an impromptu packsack. The harness material was similar to lamp-wick and was tied to the bottom corners of the sack then brought up to tie off the top, making shoulder straps. We didn't carry the packs while walking on the ice because it was easier to pull them along until we reached the portage. The surface of the ice was dry and walking wasn't too bad, yet it was smooth enough to allow the sleigh and the packs to slide along with ease.

Once again on dry land the sacks became backpacks and were carried across the portage. There was extra cargo as well; a few

Squirrel den

of the squirrel snares had already been successful. The squirrels went into a separate bag and the snares were reset. With these first furs of the season and our winter's meat we stepped out of the portage onto the ice of Little Mahigan, headed for home.

It's always so nice to be home. Clarence and I were completely exhausted from the day's events—we actually had to sneak rides on the sleigh (although we knew that Dad didn't really mind) and we had managed to do our part of the day's exercise.

While Mum organized the cabin in preparation for the evening meal, Dad went to the shack-tent and kindled a fire in the small airtight heater. This is where he skinned and stretched the squirrels into pelts. He'd made many of the stretchers from wooden crates that once held fruit and assorted vegetables. The slats were removed then carved, planed and sanded out to make thin, flat boards about sixteen inches in length, three inches at the butt and angled towards a rounded nose about one-and-a-half inches in diameter. This was one of the many tasks completed earlier in the fall to prepare for this part of the season.

The stretched pelts were fastened on with small nails and hung from the ceiling in the cabin where they were left to dry thoroughly before placing them in a cool and dry location. Here they would stay until it was time to bundle them up for sale.

Hopefully, it would stay cold and the ice would remain solid.

As evening progressed we could hear sounds like thunder coming off the lake. As the temperature dropped the ice contracted, then cracked and split in what seemed like an ongoing thunderous boom. At times these cracks ran the length of the lake and could be heard for miles. There was a strange comfort in hearing the booms, knowing it was nature's way of making ice. Bushmen would say the ice was "singing." It was a strange way to be lulled to sleep, but sleep we did—listening to the song of nature.

stolen!

November was almost gone and still there was no snow. After the initial cold snap at freeze-up it had warmed up considerably, the temperatures just slightly below freezing. It seemed a bit strange for it to be this mild for so long, but we knew Old Man Winter was just around the corner and one thing was certain, he would show up eventually.

It was decided that we would make a final trip out to Smoothstone Lake to gather the last of the staples we had left behind. Daylight hours had grown noticeably shorter so we were up and ready long before sunrise; we wanted to be at the entrance to the portage by sun-up. With the bare minimum of items necessary for survival, we started out. It was still dark out, but we could see a faint bluish tinge on the skyline to the east and it got increasingly brighter as we progressed down the lake. The timing was perfect; once we entered the portage it was just light enough to see where we were going.

In late fall and early spring, rabbit fur changes colour from brown to white and back again. This year the rabbits were near the height of their seven-year cycle and were bountiful throughout our area. In certain locations they congregated in bunches to feed off accessible young trees and bushes. Even though they tried to hide by staying still, their white coats against the greyish-brown background of earth, leafless brush and nonexistent snow made them stand out and look perfectly foolish.

We had just come out of a heavily wooded area and were crossing a short, grassy length of trail when we startled a large number of spruce grouse. They took off in a massive fluttering and beating of wings almost from under our feet—we'd scared them, sure, but I'm certain I grew an inch when I jumped! And it wasn't just me whose pulse spiked a bit higher.

It was still well before noon when we arrived at our usual rest stop along Mahigan Creek. As we got closer, we heard something making a fuss in the water. Quietly approaching, we peered over the edge. To our surprise, a number of ducks were making good use of the open water created by the moving current. Once we made ourselves known, they flew off a short distance to another spot where the stream remained open. As we took a break and sat around the fire drinking hot tea, Dad related an incident that had taken place here many years before while he was staying with Anton, the same man who once lived in the now vacant cabin on Selenite Point.

I was in my mid-teens, Dad told us, *and had just spent the winter at Mahigan with Anton Mylengar. And at Mahigan, Anton had built a small log cabin out of poplar trees. The logs were at least two feet in diameter and so large the wall height of this dwelling was just three rounds high. The cabin was about ten by ten and it had been built up in the hills on the southeast side of Little Mahigan, a half-mile in along the fresh-water spring that ran down into the lake. Anton had made another cabin too, and although it was smaller, it was unique because it had been built to span the small creek. A trapdoor in the floor opened whenever there was a need to fetch water. The water from the spring ran all year long and didn't freeze due to the thick forest and heavy moss that blanketed the area.*

After a season of trapping, Anton left for Big River to sell off the fur he had acquired, and told me to stay and look after things until he got back. It was late in the spring season when Anton left for Big River. Now, after several days in camp most of the remaining staples were gone and I realized there was no reason to stay. I rationed the food and decided to go out and see if there was any sign of Anton's return with the much-needed supplies. At the very least, someone might be near the portage at Smoothstone. So, I picked up my .22 rifle and two remaining shells, and in a gunny sack placed the last bit of salt, a small teapot with a few tea-bags, a box of matchsticks and a light blanket. A small hunting knife was strapped to my waist.

By now spring was really underway and the lake was dangerous to walk on, so I had to make my way south along the east shore and swing around the bottom of Little Mahigan to get to the portage. It took the better part of the day to get around the lake and through the portage to Smoothstone. Once there, I was really disappointed: all the north shore had started to break-up. Seeing this, I realized it would be a few days before anyone would be able to travel. Already hungry, I knew it was likely no one would show up for days. I wrestled with the idea of walking around

Smoothstone. The only problem was that if something happened along the way it would be almost impossible to get help, let alone be found.

Discouraged, I turned and started back in the direction of Mahigan. Not wanting to go back to the cabin because there was nothing to go back for but knowing that about halfway along the trail there was a partial roll of snare-wire hanging from a tree, I thought it would be good idea to get it—it would come in handy. There was also a small piece of tarp that had fallen off someone's supply bundle at some point, possibly when Anton had gone through. These two items I stuffed into the gunny sack for later use. Shortly after picking up the snare-wire and tarp I arrived at this resting spot. It was then I thought I heard ducks. And to my surprise, sure enough! I peered over the sharp edge of the bank and there, bobbing up and down on the gentle current, were several greenheads—Mallard drakes—swimming and toiling in the small river.

Well, I reacted quickly, reaching into my pocket for the second and final cartridge as I brought the gun up and fired the round already in the chamber. Miraculously, I got two ducks with one shot! The rest of them milled around for a moment, giving me the opportunity to eject and reload. At this point the Mallards decided to take off. The second and final shot caught another duck in mid-flight and it fell from the air. I pulled them into the shore with a long pole. In short order, feathers were plucked and the birds were cleaned, skewered and roasting over a rapidly-built fire. A pot of tea, fresh barbecued duck, cranberries left over from the previous year and sweetened by a season of winter's snow, a warm fire, a full belly, and the blanket and tarp for warmth and protection. Yes, things seemed to be all right with the world now.

And so the situation improved immensely. The next day while walking out to Smoothstone Lake, I noticed a few fish in the shallow creek. Great! The fish were beginning to run and spawning season had begun. So with the snare-wire and a long pole there was no lack of fresh fish to eat. The tarp made an excellent shelter and a thick bed of spruce boughs was a great mattress. Spring came in with gusto and it was warm enough to be pleasant; with no shortage of firewood and plenty to eat, living became pretty much bearable. And so it was here on this spot I stayed until the lake opened up enough that Anton was able to get back along the north end of the lake.

The fire was out now and the tea cold. It was time to get our supplies. Dad never spoke a lot about religion, even after telling us this story. Yet years later he referred to this event in particular and how the appearance of the ducks was not a coincidence; they were there to give him strength, nourishment and the encouragement he needed to carry on. Someone was looking out for him.

On the way back home we shot a few rabbits to make stew. Mum wanted to use the rabbit fur to add to the moccasins. This would keep our feet warmer and add padding to the soles. It was already quite dark out when we came off the lake and climbed the short bank to the cabin, but Dad noticed something different in the background near the meat pole, so as soon as we got to the cabin and put a light on, Dad went out to investigate. When he returned he was some upset.

At some point during the day, the bear had returned and hauled off most of our winter's meat supply. It was late in the year for a bear to be out, but because of the long fall season and moderate temperatures, it was still making the odd foraging run and this one hit the jackpot!

There was nothing that could be done right now; it would have to wait for daylight. Hopefully, we would be able to salvage some of the meat. Tomorrow would tell.

setting a fish net

Daylight came later than usual due to the heavy cloud cover. Along with the dark, menacing clouds blew a strong northeast wind directed towards the cabin, the type of wind that has a real bite to it and behind it, the chill of winter. A miserable day for a miserable task—it was time to investigate the disappearance of our meat cache.

A single hind quarter was left hanging at the meat pole and it appeared untouched, possibly because it had been tied with a rope while the others had been attached to open-ended meat hooks. The bear had made short work of dragging off the meat. It was difficult to find a trail because the bear literally carried the meat in several different directions and this in itself suggested that it was a large bear.

Dad walked in a sweeping pattern and with each pass delved deeper into the forest until he came across portions of the meat. This tracking method continued until there was no longer hope of finding anything further. The meat he did find was spoiled and no longer fit for human consumption, but it was gathered up anyway and stockpiled. And around the stockpile large rope snares were set for the bear, should it return.

After the morning's effort we sat down for a hot lunch of moose stew before carrying on with the rest of the day's activities. First thing on the agenda was to gather the fish net, ice chisel, running line and the long pole that would be used as a jigger, a kind of needle to "thread" the net under the ice. Once the gear was strapped down to the sleigh, we pulled the whole lot about fifty yards north of the cabin and about the same distance from shore. Here we chiselled a basin hole through the ice, roughly two feet square. Through this hole, the long pole was pushed entirely into the water, with a running line attached to the trailing end. As the pole floated up underneath the ice, it lined up in the general direction we wanted it to go. Using the rope, the pole was backed up a short distance underneath the surface, and then with a sharp, upward jerk using the ice for leverage, it catapulted forward. As the pole torpedoed ahead, it pulled the attached running line—measured at a hundred yards, the length of the net—along with it. The rope had an additional ten yards of slack. This was to prevent losing the end of the running line so it didn't slip through the hole; another method was to have the net ready and tie the trailing edge of the running line directly to the bridle of the net itself.

The clear ice was still relatively thin and made the pole easy to follow. After each catapult, we chiselled another hole in the ice at the front end of the pole, repeating the process over and over again until we reached the length of the net. Then we cut a final hole, the anchor hole.

The type of gill net we used was a hundred yards in length and twelve mesh in depth. It had a five-inch mesh which consti-

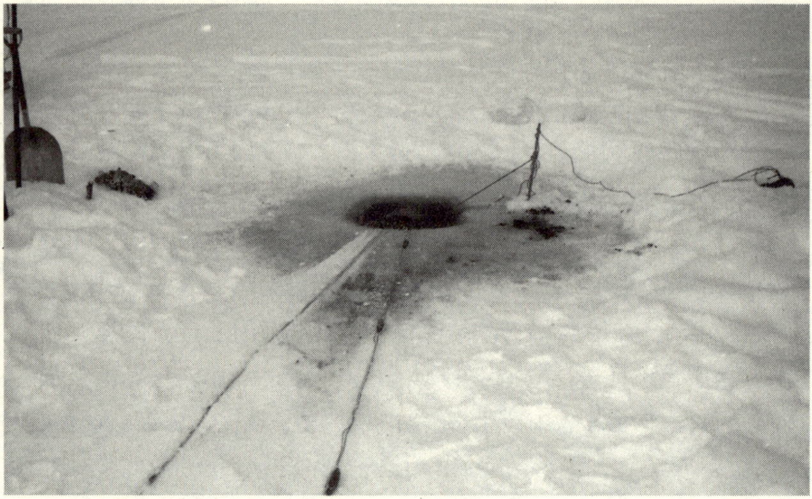

Checking the net

tuted a depth of about five feet and a short bridle on each end, free from webbing used to attach the running or anchor lines. To draw the net under the ice, the running line was pulled from the anchor hole end, and the net was tied to a rock that was then sunk to keep the net down so the floats wouldn't freeze against the ice. Anchors were attached at each end so the net could be retrieved later. The running line was then untied and reattached again when the net was fished.

There are other types of jiggers where all you need is the basin and anchor holes, but this was all we had and it worked fine as long as the ice wasn't too thick. The fishing in this area was ideal. We fished and reset the net often throughout the winter months as the need arose, exchanging the net for the running line when we had enough fish and securing it to the anchor lines for future use. Now, with the net set it was time to get back to the cabin and do the general chores.

The wind never let up at all and it got colder as the day progressed. Darkness came early and so did sleep.

the bear

Startled out of a sound sleep! Loud noises from somewhere in the forest. It was like someone or something splitting wood or banging logs together, crashing through the bush. We thought for a moment we were in the midst of a storm until we realized there was no wind. What could it be? It didn't take long before we were all up and dressed, but because it was still dark out all we could do was wait for daylight to come to find out what it was all about.

The heater was stoked with fresh kindling and firewood. As the heat radiated across the room it took the morning chill out of the cabin. The glow from the coal oil lamp pushed away the darkness and the light and heat brought a sense of warmth and security as we watched daybreak slowly take shape on the horizon. As soon as it was light enough to see we ventured outside. The racket was coming from the direction of the pile of meat.

Dad grabbed his rifle and went to investigate. With fear we watched as the forest engulfed him. For a long time it seemed there was no sound when suddenly a gunshot rang out! Muffled

Us boys and the bear

as it was by the dense bush, it still echoed out across the lake. All was silent after that. We waited in suspense for quite some time until, finally, Dad entered the clearing and came strolling up with news: the bear—and a large one at that—had indeed returned. It had been caught in one of the rope snares. Now that the bear situation was under control, the excitement abated and we sat down for breakfast to plan out the rest of the day.

We were almost finished the morning meal when there was a knock on the door. Clarence and I scrambled to the safety of our beds while Dad answered. It was our neighbour, George. Mum poured him a cup of fresh-perked coffee off the cookstove as he sat down. He'd been out along the lake when he'd heard a gunshot, and being curious—knowing that bullets were precious and you didn't waste ammunition on just anything—he'd been certain something was up. Because he was only a short distance away he'd decided to come and help out if necessary, and visit at the very least—for that in itself was long overdue.

Dad and the stretched bear hide

After catching up on the latest "local" news and the ground we had covered since our last visit, they went to skin out the bear and decided to drag it back to the cabin. The entrails were removed to shed weight and then, rope around the bear's neck, it was dragged back in behind the cabin. Here the hide was removed and rolled up temporarily to keep it from drying until it could be stretched. The large amount of fat on the animal was trimmed off and set into a tub. When there was no more that could be done with the carcass, it was taken out onto the ice and a hole was chiselled through that the carcass could freeze in. This would hopefully attract fur-bearing animals and maybe there would be another opportunity to use the rifle.

Dad built a fire in the firepit. Mum filled a large aluminium cookpot with chunks of bear fat and hung it from the wire hook above the hot coals. The fat was boiled and rendered down to a liquid, then cooled a bit before being poured through a cloth sieve. Mum molded tinfoil into small squares with sides, and the rendered fat was poured into these pans, allowing them to cool and harden into white blocks. They would be used as shortening for making bannock, bread and also for frying. It was my job to stay and be a nuisance to Mum while she attended to this task.

Meanwhile, Dad, George and Clarence went out to check the net after taking the bear carcass out; they were gone for a couple of hours before returning with a small tub of fish: northern pike and whitefish. There was pickerel around, but none had been netted overnight. As a rule we checked the net every second day, so the catch was good considering the net had been in for only a night. This told us the location was ideal and would give us a steady supply of fresh fish.

The afternoon turned out to be very mild and pleasant, so another fire was made in the firepit outside. A stockpile of seasoned birch had been set aside for these special occasions, the bark trimmed off to prevent black smoke from tainting the flavour or creating creosote and thus spoiling the meal. Because it is a hardwood, the birchwood left a hot bed of lasting coals after the flames died down. The large frying pan was set over the coals and a block of rendered bear fat thrown in. Once the fish were cleaned and washed, the fillets were ready to be fried. They were placed in the hot frying pan and soon cooked to a golden brown. Fresh bannock and pan-fried fillets mixed with the aroma of light smoke from seasoned birch is a great meal in the wild outdoors. For dessert, Mum made applesauce from dried apples, which was then generously applied in large amounts over the bannock.

Lunch finished, George made ready to leave. Dad put the rest of the fish in a bag for him and Mum tucked a jar of the fresh applesauce into his pocket; this brought a smile to George's face.

It was so good to see George again and hear that he was making out just fine. Dad really appreciated the extra help that day.

After George left, Dad donned his jacket, picked up the packsack and left for the north end of the lake to check the squirrel sets. The rest of the afternoon was uneventful and things quieted down enough for Mum to work on her jigsaw puzzle. As she fit a section of puzzle together, Mum shared a story:

> *There was once a small Indian village located nearby. The whole village was wiped out in an epidemic that raged through this region, leaving no survivors. I'm not sure what disease caused this catastrophe, but I think it was smallpox. A few of these tragic events took place over the years, but there was one in particular that took place during 1781-1782. Smallpox and famine raged throughout the land and it's estimated over half of the Cree perished in this one epidemic alone.*
>
> *A more recent one took place in 1918. A severe influenza epidemic attacked all ethnic groups and claimed Anna, Dad's grandmother, among many thousands of others. In turn, many of the small Indian villages that were sporadically dotted across the land disappeared, in particular throughout our region of Northern Saskatchewan.*
>
> The Indian village that had once been nearby had disappeared completely into the unknown. Nature and time and forest growth had reclaimed it all. To our young minds this was mind-boggling and more than a little frightening, to say the least.

Daylight faded just as Dad returned from the trapline. He had a packsack full of fur. Some needed thawing and would have to wait until the next day before cleaning and stretching; those that weren't frozen were cleaned and stretched right away. He had seen beaver swimming at the small river to the north. They had built their lodge along the deepest part of the river and would thus have access to open water for at least a few more days so Dad would wait until the ice formed around the lodge before making an attempt to snare them.

In the next few days he needed to make a few more runs to establish the trapline. Each run would be checked on a regular basis, especially on warmer days, to prevent any unnecessary suffering of the animal. There would be times when it would be impossible to check the trapline due to bad weather, but as a rule animals don't move around much then anyway. Dad explained to us the need to check the line frequently, not only to be humane, but also to prevent the fur from being damaged by other animals and make any catches easier to find.

Over the next several days daylight soon became darkness. Our days were full getting the trapline set out. Any spare time was used to stretch fur, and this included the bearskin. The net had to be checked every second day and since it was bringing in just enough fish to eat it remained in the water. And don't forget all the regular chores required to keep the cabin warm and all of us fed! These few days certainly answered the age-old bushman's question: "What do you do with all your time?"

November was gone, but what would December be like? Where was the snow? Was nature playing a trick on us? A season like this came along only once in a blue moon, but we knew one thing for sure: nature has a real sense of humour and at times it can take you completely by surprise.

the arrival of winter

It was like an enormous groan. It started out slowly sometime in the very early hours of the morning, just after midnight. It had been calm and real quiet out until then. Now, though, there was a distinct stirring of sound invading the privacy of the silence, its tempo slowly increasing with each passing moment until it could contain itself no longer. Then with a loud moan the storm unleashed its pent-up fury into a giant roar. And the wind came—our first storm of the season; winter had arrived!

We wondered why it seemed to be daylight sooner than expected. Yet the light progressed slowly; it seemed to be pre-dawn for the longest time. The wind howled past our small home and some of the heavy gusts literally made the cabin tremble. The draft on the stove whistled with each passing blast of wind, making the stovepipes rattle against the supports. It was really loud inside as the storm raged on. When it was light enough to finally see, we knew that the day would be spent inside and there would be no venturing out at all. The snow was coming down heavy and with blinding force as the wind drove it forward.

The lake was a complete whiteout and we couldn't see much of anything, so there would certainly be no travelling until it blew over. Storms like this can carry on for several days before petering out, but most last only a day or two, and we hoped for the latter. We now understood why daylight had seemed to come so quick; what light there was reflected off all the snow, giving pale illumination.

The day went on with the usual chores and the fur that had thawed overnight could now be skinned and stretched. Mum took the opportunity to complete our wrap-arounds and we could hardly wait to try them out in the new snow.

We had an a.m. radio that we listened to, mostly tuned to our favourite station out of Prince Albert. We would turn it on sparingly to conserve the batteries, but on days like this we made an exception. Even though there was a lot of static and it was very difficult to hear everything being said, we were able to pick out the weather report and it sounded promising. To get reception, a wire had been run from the radio and connected to a long wire antenna outside. The antenna was strung between two poles, one on each side of the yard. This set-up worked very well and the radio was good company; it helped us keep in touch with the outside world. There was a program broadcast on CKBI Prince Albert on weekdays at 5:45 p.m. that we listened to all the time: "The Northern News." People would call in and leave a message, and the station would broadcast it to family and friends out on the trapline. It was something we tried not to miss and always listened with a great deal of interest. We too received a message this way every once in awhile, reminding us that we hadn't been forgotten and creating a lot of excitement. Even if the message wasn't for us, we enjoyed listening to every bit of information relayed. And so we were kept informed about who was on the trapline, what furs were being caught and the price of each pelt sold at the fur-buyer level. It really was a lifeline–a type of "moccasin communication," if you will.

The hours passed and evening came. The wind let up some, but the snow continued to fall long into the night. As we lay in our beds listening to the blizzard outside we were content, knowing the cabin would keep us safe and warm. The storm raged on for another day and we made ourselves as useful around the limits of the cabin as space and time allowed. It was time spent getting caught up on personal thoughts and hobbies, and general maintenance and repair around the cabin. One of the positive aspects of times like this was the opportunities we had to listen to Mum and Dad as they talked with each other. They discussed plans for the future and the avenues they could pursue to achieve their goals—many were more than likely just dreams, but every dream has the possibility of being made real in due time, depending only on your desire to remain true to their focus. Their conversations during these times remain ingrained in me today; the values taught at a very young age, values to be proud of.

At some point during the night the wind stopped and by morning the snow had played itself out as well. The snow-filled storm clouds had blown themselves out and morning brought an absolutely brilliant scene, a perfect winter wonderland: the sun peeking over the far hill against the deep blue of the sky, all the landscape covered in a white, fluffy blanket of pure white snow; the evergreens held out their branches as if gently cradling the precious powdery gift from above. There was not a track to be seen anywhere and in the stillness time stopped in tranquil beauty. Standing there at the window, we were fascinated by the awesome display before us. Suddenly, a lone wolf call broke the silence, the echo reverberating across the hills to vanish into the distance. It was like an alarm clock and nature and all its inhabitants woke up. Yes, indeed, December had come in like a lion, or should I say, a wolf!

The arrival of the snow meant it would be a marathon to get out to check the trapline. All the snares would have to be reset as they would be all buried under more than a foot of newly fallen snow. Dad gathered the necessary items he'd need for survival while out checking the line. In the packsack he carried a wool blanket, an extra pair of woollen socks (both wrapped in a waterproof bag), the trusty teapot, tea bags, a bit of sugar, salt and matches. The dry goods and matches were also placed in a waterproof container. He also carried a small medicine kit containing a few painkillers and a roll of bandages. For trapping supplies, he had a small axe and ready-made snares for squirrel, fox, coyote and lynx. All these items were kept down to a bare minimum in order to keep the pack light and still have room for fur.

Because he would be using snowshoes for the first time this year the sleigh would stay at camp. Breaking a new trail would be hard enough without dragging the sleigh behind—it would only slow him down. There was a lot of ground to cover and he needed to move as quickly as possible. With his packsack on and carrying only his .22 rimfire, he set a course for the far shore. The first leg was through the portage at the northeast end of the lake and along the north shore of the second lake where there was a beaver lodge to check. This was also the spot from which we'd hauled out the moose meat earlier. From that point there were several squirrel dens to check.

The route would eventually take him out onto the water of Big Mahigan along the northwest shore. The trail then doubled back to the narrows. Once at the narrows it was a short distance across to the return along the south shore. All along this route were a variety of sets, consisting of mainly snares. There were a few small coni-bear traps set out along the river for smaller fur such as mink and weasel. The area contained two types of fur: short-hair fur—beaver, muskrat, mink, weasel, squirrel, marten and otter; and the long- haired fur—bear, wolves, coyote, a variety of fox, fisher and sometimes lynx. There was talk of the odd skunk and even the infamous wolverine, but they were few and far between and there had been no recent sightings, at least in this particular neck of the woods.

after the storm

After the storm there were plenty of tasks that needed immediate attention, some more so than others, and we started on the ones that took priority. This was great! Now we had the opportunity to try on our new wrap-arounds and they were just awesome, comfortable and warm.

The water barrel had been neglected during the storm and needed filling, but first thing on the agenda was to clear a path to the water hole, scrape away the snow and chisel through to open water. Once the ice was removed several trips would be required to replenish the water barrel. The path to the outhouse and woodpile needed clearing as well.

Once these chores were done it was time to challenge the hill behind the cabin. Pieces of cardboard worked great as sleds, but it took a few runs before the trail was packed enough to have a good ride. Eventually we succeeded, or should I say, *I* succeeded, since my brother thought it was his duty to teach me the meaning of the word "snowplough," and rammed me downhill at a dead run! At any rate, we could almost make it to the cabin. We called this Mahigan Mountain, even though the hill was quite small. What a great way to enjoy the snow!

Mum had her work cut out for her. Today she was washing all our clothes and bedding, which would keep her busy most of the day. With Mum tied up with her task, Clarence and I decided to go on a little adventure of our own—or at least *he* thought so! Still, I went along with it because it would be a good way to break-in our brand new wrap-arounds. We put on our winter parkas and off we went, slowly making our way along the shoreline in the direction of the portage to the south. It was fun walking and making crazy designs in the fresh snow.

It was a beautiful day, the temperature hovering around zero Fahrenheit. There was no wind at all and the air smelled fresh and clean. It was neat to see all the different tracks that had begun to materialize along the bank and into the bush. Snow birds, weasel, squirrel, snowshoe rabbit and several chicken tracks, most likely a flock of spruce grouse as the partridge stayed further in and the ptarmigan were not yet in from the barren lands. The tracks from the grouse led out from holes in the snow where they had plummeted beneath to keep out of the storm and stay warm. Emerging from their cosy dens, they made funny patterns in the soft powder as they ploughed along, feeding off small twigs and frozen buds. The rabbits fared slightly better since they were able to hop across the top with their large hind feet and didn't sink in as much. Even though all the tracks were fresh the only thing we spotted was the snow birds. These tiny birds dashed in and out along the lakeshore, staying just ahead of us, feeding on seeds from the many small trees growing along the bank.

It was surprising how fast time went by and we soon found ourselves at the entrance to the portage. After fooling around for a short while in the snow we decided to carry on to George's cabin, now only a short distance away. As we walked up we could see fresh footprints at the water hole and tracks leading away to the south, along the shore towards the river. When we came off the lake and strolled up the path to his cabin we could see smoke rising from the stovepipes and the snow had been well packed down in front.

We called out to announce our arrival, "Hello, George! Are you home?" and knocked on the door to be sure, but there was no answer, so we stepped inside where it was yet nice and warm, though a bit dark. It took a few moments for our eyes to adjust in the dim lighting, and soon we could see just fine. The interior smelled like a mixture of pitch from the spruce logs, woodsmoke, fur pelts…and something else? Doughnuts! George had made a batch of deep-fried doughnuts before heading out on his line. He had placed them on a rack to cool and covered them with cheesecloth. Their aroma was very fresh so George had only been gone a short while. Once we warmed up and each ate a doughnut, it was time to get back home. We felt a bit guilty for taking and eating them, even though George had told us we were welcome to come over any time and if he was away just to make ourselves at home. We felt those tasty morsels fit that invitation, and regardless of the twinge in conscience, took one more each for the trail.

It was mid-afternoon by the time Clarence and I approached home. The sun had gone behind the hills to the west and was casting long shadows on the lake like fingers slowly extending, reaching for the far shore with each passing minute. We were almost home when Mum came around one of the points along the shore. When we were spotted she stopped and waited for us until we arrived. She had been so busy working on the clothes and chores she didn't realize we had gone until she went out to hang the laundry on the clothesline. It wasn't difficult to find our tracks, seeing that they were the only two going south, so she knew we had gone for a visit. Anyway, she didn't say much except, *"Eehee-ah-wuh! Was-tuh-gatts!"* Cree Indian slang meaning "I just can't believe it!" but she did look genuinely happy to see us. Years later both George and Mum remembered this day: the fright we had given Mum, who was then overjoyed to see the two of us safe. And George, on his return, was thrilled to find small footprints—and four missing doughnuts, though we were quickly forgiven. By the way, the wrap-around moccasins proved faultless in the snow.

The shadow had reached the far side of the lake by now and the first shades of dusk had begun to form. It was like a dark window blind slowly being pulled down until it reached the bottom, closing out all light. When it became dark enough, the coal oil lamp was lit and the wick trimmed, bringing light to the cabin but also making it instantly dark beyond the windows. This was always the darkest part of the evening until the moon was high enough to brighten up the area. Mum started preparing the evening meal. We expected Dad home shortly since he usually tried to be back by nightfall or shortly thereafter. With the extra work the snowstorm had created it would take quite a bit longer to re-establish each run on the trapline. Because of this, Mum surmised Dad would be later than usual, so we carried on with eating supper. The blankets had been drying on the short clothesline along the back wall for the better part of the day and they were now dry. So after clearing up the dishes Mum made our beds for the night.

By now it was getting late and there was still no sign of Dad. Clarence and I were put to bed, but there was no sleeping. We knew Mum was getting worried. As time dragged on the uncertainty increased, adding to the worry. Each run on the trapline was geared for a winter's day of travel, now long since passed. Mum put a candle in the window in hopes that its light would give Dad direction. The radio played softly in the background until it became a distraction and was switched off. The silence was nearly deafening. The only sound was the occasional opening and closing of the cabin door when Mum went outside to listen for any sign of Dad. She stayed out for long periods of time until the cold night air forced her back inside the warm cabin.

All through the night she continued this vigil, outside to listen, back inside to stoke up the fire, set a new candle at the window and then trim the wick on the oil lamp. To ease her mind, she worked on the puzzle she'd started at freeze-up, but only for a short time as the nervous tension built up until she couldn't sit still any longer. This scenario repeated itself over and over again as the night wore on. There were times when she heard wolves howling and their echo bounced across the hills—the cold, still air magnifying the lonely sound. There was the odd rumble as the ice adjusted to the added weight of the snow. Daylight wasn't far off and Mum would begin a search then—in the meantime she gathered the necessary clothes and gear needed for the trail.

The light of dawn crested the horizon and full daylight came. Mum was almost ready to go when we were startled by a noise outside. We sat bolt upright. The sound had our complete attention. Our eyes were riveted on the door. Suddenly, it swung open and there was Dad, covered over with a build-up of frost from the cold outside air but otherwise all right.

Once Dad entered he confirmed that he was fine and that in general it had been a very good run, but what a night and what an experience. And for us, what a relief!

the hunt

After setting the packsack down, Dad took off his parka and went directly to the stove to suck in some much needed heat. Mum quickly poured a coffee for him, and after a few tentative sips of the hot liquid we could tell he had started to thaw from the inside out. Dad then told us what had happened to him from the time he'd left the previous morning.

It was a joy breaking trail on the season's first trip on snow-shoes and he'd made good time crossing the lake over to the portage at the north end. He decided to clean all the fur that hadn't frozen and pick them up at designated spots on his re-turn. At each beaver lodge the snow had to be cleared away from where the sets had been placed and the ice that had accumulated in the holes over the past couple of days had to be chopped out before pulling out the snare pole. This process would be repeat-ed many times throughout the winter months. At any rate, the first beaver lodge produced a medium-sized beaver, and using his trapper's knowledge the snares were reset. This decision was based on a few things: the number of lodges in the area, the size of the lodge, and what had been harvested. By and large, whether or not to reset a snare is at the trapper's discretion, but it's crucial for a trapper to govern his trapline respectfully and with proper management to maintain a healthy and sustainable environment year after year, and vitally important to ensure the trapper's well-being and continued livelihood.

After the snares were reset, Dad skinned the beaver and put the pelt in a secure location. Then it was off through the portage to check the squirrel snares. The catch was very good—which was surprising—due to the large amount of snow that had fallen, although where the squirrel dens were located the forest was thick and much of the snow didn't make it all the way down. Still, it took some time to go through all the sets even though it was just a short hop over to the bigger lake.

Once everything had been reset and the work done, it was onward along the north shore to another huge beaver lodge; this one produced one large beaver and one kit. From here the pelts would have to be packed and carried to the narrows where the bigger part of the lake started. There they'd be left in a safe place until they could be retrieved on the return trip. The beaver carcasses Dad left against a tree along the bank, and small poles and sticks were placed to form a cubby. Snares were set in front of the opening for fox, fisher, coyote or maybe the odd lynx. There were squirrels sets along the way to re-establish as well.

As the journey proceeded to the narrows, the fur was hidden in various spots and now Dad was at the big lake. There were several sets along the west and north shores. Usually Dad would do this in one run and then backtrack, but when he was ready to return from the top of the run, a movement caught his attention—something large and dark against the backdrop of the eastern shoreline. Dad mulled it over. Because the last few sets had produced nothing, his packsack was light and it was still early enough in the day to check it out. If he went to investigate, his return trip would be on the south side of Big Mahigan and although that would mean he'd be late getting back home, it could be done. This would also be a benefit as the south run would not then have to be checked the following day. And so, decision made, Dad made a beeline for the east shore. The only audible sound came from the *swish-swish* of the snowshoes carving a gentle path with each stride.

It was a perfect winter day—the sun shining, no wind and the temperature a few degrees below zero. The scenery was absolutely breathtaking. It wasn't long before the southeast shoreline grew clear. The large black object now started to move—a moose! It was feeding on the small, tender branches sticking out all along the shore. It was small, but at this time of year the bull moose start to lose their horns, which makes it difficult to tell whether it's male or female until you're close enough.

Dad continued his forward progress. To keep from being detected he stayed close to shore, blending in with the shadow from the trees. Finally he stopped and waited for the moose to come to him. He was close enough to see that it was a dry cow, a cow moose that had not had a calf in the past year. A small creek flowed out of the hills between them, and just about the time a clean shot could be taken, the moose turned, disappearing into the bush along the south side of the creek.

Dad knew the area well; there was a small bluff a short distance in. There the creek doubled back on itself as it went around this higher point of land. He figured the moose would continue to feed along the creek and if he could to get to that bluff in time there was a possibility he might be close enough for an accurate shot.

He untied the snowshoes and left them behind to eliminate the possibility of them bumping against a tree and alerting the moose. There was no sound as he scurried through the soft snow, which acted like a thick blanket and muffled any further noise. Soon the bluff came into view. It was a slow climb up the east side, one step and a pause to look around, then another step. It seemed to take a long time, but eventually the bit of high ground was reached. And just as he crested the small knoll he heard popping sounds, very close. The moose was breaking off branches and munching on the frozen twigs, and its path led directly past the bluff. Dad had to wait until the moose was even closer since all he carried was the .22 rimfire. Even though a long-rifle cartridge was in the chamber, he still needed a good, clean shot.

Dad got comfortable, making a nest in the snow, and with his back against a tree for camouflage, he waited. The sun started its downward plunge towards the southwest and the long shadows of late afternoon were forming. He knew it would be a late one today and normally wouldn't have pursued an animal this far from home, but meat was a necessity after the bear's Thanksgiving dinner and he wasn't about to turn down an opportunity when it presented itself. Now that the cold weather was here there was no worry about the meat spoiling. He could haul back a portion each time he checked this side of the trapline.

The sun was almost down when the moose walked clear from the willow thicket that invaded both sides of the small creek. As the animal passed him it was almost close enough to touch. The small rifle slowly followed the animal and sighted in just below and behind the left ear.

Time stopped.

With long years of practise in the bush, plus the gifts of a sharpshooter, Dad was in no panic and no rush; the rifle waited, unwavering, as his finger gently squeezed the trigger.

Pop! Very little sound came from the small game rifle as the trees swallowed the sharp report. And even this sound didn't matter for the bullet found its mark and the animal became a family's food supply.

Now there *was* a rush—to get the animal cleaned and quartered. First thing to do was go pick up the snowshoes and packsack. Once the gear was collected Dad made a trail in by snowshoe along the creek. This direct route was just a stone's throw from the lake. With a sharp knife and a lot of experience, the meat was soon ready to be hung. Dad used fox snares to suspend the meat from a pole placed across two spruce trees, the meat covered with spruce boughs to protect it from small animals and birds—especially ravens, the only scavenger that stays the winter.

In the midst of the evergreens and willows crowding the edge of the creek was a substantial amount of dry wood. After collecting a few of these dry timbers, it wasn't long before Dad had a roaring fire and put on the teapot. It was actually a nice spot and just high enough to look west across the expanse of Big Mahigan, the setting sun on the horizon and beyond the treeline, Mahigan Lake and home.

Refreshed after tea and lunch, he quickly gathered his gear together and made ready for the trek back to camp. Daylight was fading fast and Dad wanted to be on the lake before darkness settled in. It would get quite dark out, but only for a short while until the moon came up. The moon would give enough light to see by and it wouldn't take long to cross the lake and get home.

But just as he was about to leave, all hell broke loose in the stillness—wolves began to howl from every direction and very close! They must have been following the cow moose, heavy into hunt mode—and obviously very hungry, for they surrounded the kill site and continued to circle and howl.

Just then it was like someone blew out a candle and the last shred of daylight blinked on the western horizon and was gone. Dad made a quick decision to stay put. He rekindled the fire and piled the dry wood high to encourage a huge blaze. This cast a considerable amount of light which made it relatively easy to gather more firewood.

And it wasn't just wolves in the vicinity, there were other sounds as well—and they all came from the dark just beyond the firelight. Something large was moving around out there. All would be silent for awhile and then the commotion started up all over again. The wolves continued to howl and every once in a while Dad could hear loud rasping grunts, smashing bush and wild yelps coming from just past the circle of light.

The campfire's brilliant blaze made the darkness even darker and more foreboding than ever; the flames flickered designs against shadowy, snow-covered trees, and the uncertainty of not knowing what was happening out there only made the situation worse. During the short intervals when everything was quiet, Dad would quickly venture out and drag in more dry wood to replenish the fire. A few times, and only briefly, he could see what seemed to be a large shape moving back and forth. It would stop for short periods of time before disappearing into the blackness of the night, only to reappear again in the midst of howling wolves, which had by now completely surrounded the small bluff. The small-calibre rifle seemed terribly inadequate and Dad thought longingly of his big rifle back home. However, there was nothing that could be done now except keep the fire going and stay in the safety of the light while the drama unfolded around him.

The moon had been up for a while now but remained hidden by a small bank of clouds that had formed at nightfall. Dad was glad when it chose to break free and it seemed to him exceptionally large in the frosty night air. It soon cleared its dark curtain and continued to rise, casting a dull glow tinged with yellow across the landscape, the effect eerie.

There was another moment of quiet then things became real serious: a huge eruption of noise, crashing brush, yelps and bellows then silence again. There was the sound of heavy wheezing amid growls—and then nothing. That was enough for Dad and he fired a couple of precious rounds into the night air. The report from the .22-calibre bullet seemed extremely loud in the cold, still air and whether or not it helped the situation, there was no further sound of action from the battle that had raged on for what seemed like an eternity. Speculation ended and growing realization became fact; there was, at the very least, one more moose in close proximity and the pack of wolves was intent on making a kill. Nothing was going to get in the way of their meal. Why the moose chose to keep so close to Dad's fire is a bit of a mystery; perhaps it somehow sensed it had a better chance of survival by staying as near as it did or maybe it was just the final location of its last stand.

As the moon made its wayward journey across the heavens, the yellow tinge vanished, leaving a pure white glow and allowing Dad to see reasonably well. Except for the crackling of the fire, all became very quiet as the night wore on. Now that things had calmed down Dad was able to make tea and a bit of hot lunch. The area around the tree where he'd taken refuge was by now well-packed and the limbs were dry and free of snow. The heat radiated into the small, cleared opening between the roots and lower branches where he sat, and it was reasonably warm and comfortable, so, topping off the fire with more dry wood, Dad wrapped himself in the wool blanket and dozed off.

When you spend a night out in the woods under these conditions all you get are short power naps and then you wake up chilled when the fire winds down. In most cases, you tend to cook on one side and freeze on the other, but it wasn't too bad for Dad since the hot fire had warmed the base of the tree real well and the wool blanket did a great job in fending off the cold.

The stars followed a respectable distance behind the moon as it made its arc across the northern hemisphere. The further the moon moved to the west, the brighter the stars became until the whole universe lit up in a magnificent display of natural wonder. It seemed to Dad he could reach out and grab hold of a star. With the night now clear and calm, the smoke and small burning embers from the fire went straight skywards, the sparks twinkling until they burnt themselves out.

There was no further interruption for the rest of the night and the sun would soon send the first rays of dawn to brighten the skyline. With this in mind, the gear was stowed back in the packsack, the snowshoes tied and, trusty rifle in hand, Dad followed yesterday's snowshoe trail back out to the lake. Since this was the end of a run on the trapline, there wouldn't be as many sets to check on the return.

There were no beavers on the south shore since the lake was too shallow; it wasn't until somewhere near the southeast shore that the lake deepened. This stretch of shoreline was straighter so took less time to walk. By the time Dad approached the first set of snares, there was enough daylight to see clearly. There was a small island just off the narrows and this is what Dad aimed for. In the summer, the island was used by cormorants, a large black duck that spends the summer competing with pelicans for fish. Now, though, it was empty bar the odd tall tree standing bare and dead, splattered white from many years of bird crap.

After cutting across the north end of this tiny island it was a short walk to where the previous day's fur had been stored. Thankfully, the cache was still safe and secure. A short jaunt over to a secluded bay where the last beaver set was completed the run. This lodge produced another beaver of medium size. Dad attached a rope around the beaver's neck and pulled it because his packsack was now fully laden and heavy with fur. From there it was a short walk over to the portage and into Little Mahigan.

It was full daylight when Dad rounded the point, the cabin and the inviting smoke rising from the stovepipes a welcome sight. When he was close enough he could see the still-lit candle at the window.

aftermath

Dad may have saved half a day's journey by completing the south run on Big Mahigan the night before, but it certainly was a tough way to gain the extra time. And now there was the fur to prepare, so the rest of the day fell to a mixture of assorted tasks: preparing the furs, skinning, flushing the fat off the pelts and stretching them skin-side out to dry. And while all this was taking place, a pot had been on the stove, slowly churning small, cubed moose meat into tender morsels of delight that would melt in your mouth. A small portion of our dwindling supply of potatoes was added to the stewing meat and a can of vegetables completed the mix.

It was late afternoon by the time all the fur had been prepared and the equipment was washed and put away. Without anything further on the agenda we sat down for an early supper. We dug into the stew with ravenous appetites, mostly due to the fact that the aroma from the stew had been tickling our nostrils all day. Now, after all the events of the past few days, the trapline was in order and current, our winter's meat supply re-established, chores done for the day, hot food filled our bellies and we were exhausted from the last two days of labour; it was lights out.

Morning came crisp and clear, no wind and cold enough to have a real bite to it. The net had to be fished today. It was one of the first things on the morning's to-do list. As we left the protection of the warm cabin and stepped out into the cold, frosty air, a shiver ran the whole length of our frames as our bodies adjusted to the difference of temperature. When we exhaled, our breath came out in a cloud of white frost that hung in the air. Clarence challenged me to a duel to see who could blow the farthest, measured by the distance of the white fog we were able to produce. He won!

We didn't have an outdoor thermometer, but the radio weather report mentioned some areas nearest us had dipped to 50 below zero—cold enough to make the ice sing again. With the gear ready we left to fish the net. It was really neat to see the fish come out of the hole as the net was being pulled. Dad used a fish hook specially made for taking fish out of a gill net, and after the fish were taken out and put into the wood fish box, the job of pulling in the net continued until the full length of the net was checked.

The rough fish in this particular case were suckers and these were tossed aside and used as bait on the trapline. When it was this cold out the fish didn't take long to freeze. The ones left out in the open air flopped only a few times before freezing solid. The rest in the box remained thawed enough to fillet when we got back to the cabin. Today it was Mum and us boys' turn on the running line to pull the net back under the ice. Dad made sure the net went back in straight, clean and free from debris and knots or tangles that might have been missed when it was drawn out. After tying the anchors at each hole we trudged back into camp, pulling the sleigh with a few good eating fish. There was a good supply of whitefish and northern pike. And there were even a couple of pickerel in today's catch. Our midday meal was freshly caught fish, canned corn and brown beans, along with fresh bannock. There was also cranberry dessert!

Dad and Clarence went across the lake, checking the line along the small creek. It was well worth the effort as this produced a fisher, a large male mink and a few squirrels. On the way back they filled a jug of spring water and cut a dry pole for firewood. It was always a treat to drink the spring water that always ran cold and clear regardless of the weather. The rest of the day was spent gathering more firewood and restocking the woodpile. Mum and I looked after the affairs of the cabin. Mum mixed up dry ingredients and baked bannock and put the white beans that had been soaking overnight on the stove to cook.

While this was taking place, I was busy making tiny snares for the mice that had decided to invade our territory. Mice had made a trail alongside the cabin and this is where I set the tiny snares. Everyone had a little time to spend on their own today. Dad had a few aircraft magazines he looked over and spent the last part of the afternoon dreaming about buying an airplane one day. Mum had accumulated a number of true romance magazines and was reading through the short stories, probably for the second or maybe even third time. Meanwhile, my brother and I played with an old deck of cards. Clarence was trying to show me some newfangled game he'd dreamed up, but to his consternation it was going nowhere! His patience was a mite thin even at this early age. Yet it was nice to have a day that ended this way.

It warmed up a considerable amount overnight and daylight brought with it a beautiful winter day and moderate temperatures. With an early start all of us headed out for a meat run to the far shores of Big Mahigan. It would be a straight walk there; we would check the beaver lodges and other sets on the return as time allowed. This was great since I didn't get out very often and it was always an adventure no matter how far we travelled. Mum and Dad had snowshoes and a sleigh each. The snowshoe trail had frozen hard and was easy for us boys to walk on, but we still managed to snag a few rides whenever the occasion presented itself, which became quite regular as the journey progressed. Poor Mum. We didn't dare pick on Dad.

We approached the frozen creek a bit before noon. This was where the trail led into the bush where the meat was. The wolf activity in the area was already evident, even before reaching the creek. The snow had been completely packed down by the footprints of a large number of timber wolves. We didn't know what to expect when we arrived—we even wondered if there would be anything left for us. As we entered the mouth of the tiny creek and made our way up the trail, we could see moose tracks scattered among a vast amount of wolf tracks.

And now that it was broad daylight we could see the scenario that had unfolded the other night. The signs written in the snow were quite clear and told of the unfortunate demise of a moose under attack by a pack of wolves. You could see where they had surrounded the huge animal on several occasions and where it had made a valiant effort to fight off the demons of the night. But, slowly exhausted from the constant barrage of the unrelenting wolves, it slowly succumbed to defeat. The wolves had continued their onslaught, attacking the moose from behind with their razor sharp canines, ultimately severing its main tendons. Once the animal lost the ability to stand, it fell on its back legs but continued to fight for freedom by pulling itself along with its front legs through the underbrush. There was a steady stream of blood marking the trail of death, and as the moose crawled along, the wolves had leapt onto the animal's back and started feeding on the hump just behind its neck. This carried on until the life was literally drained from the animal and the saga of another wolf kill at last came to an end.

Soon after we came upon the remains of the carcass and the story written in blood was confirmed. We looked on in silence, speaking not a word, shocked at the brutality of the scene before us, yet fully understanding the wolves' need to survive just as we did. We carried on to our own meat supply to find that we were in luck—it had not been touched.

It was a quiet walk back home, each in our own thoughts, pondering the events that had taken place just days before. The sets along the route home were empty and with nothing further to slow us we made good time on our return. The closing minutes of daylight were upon us when we stepped onto the ice of Little Mahigan and from the point we could barely make out the cabin in the dusk, but it was a welcome sight and our pace livened up for the home stretch.

The cabin was still warm. The lantern was lit and the ashes in the stove were stirred to find the still-live coals buried beneath. Birchbark and kindling were added to get the fire going and soon it was roaring, causing the stovepipes to turn a bright cherry red from the heat of the flames. The teapot and yesterday's beans were set on the hot stove to warm the evening meal while we sat at the kitchen table, waiting patiently. Meals like homemade soups and stews always taste better the next day and being in the cold all day certainly complemented this fact.

We were almost done eating when we heard a message coming over the radio on "Northern News": "Here's a message going out to Jim, Flora and the boys at Mahigan Lake: 'Will be arriving in the next few days to start fishing.' This message is coming from the Schleogles at Smoothstone Lake." Frank was coming in with his team of horses to commercial fish the big lake.

Now this caused a great deal of excitement since Frank would be making several trips to transport his catch to the fish plant in Big River. Frank was always keen for company and an extra hand on these trips. This worked out well for everyone because it was an opportunity for Dad to sell the fur we'd caught and replenish our fast-depleting stock, especially vegetables. The potatoes, carrots, turnips and onions were all but gone, with the exception of a few potatoes, but even the bottom of the barrel could be seen with those. Not to mention that this trip in would be a pre-Christmas run, which was obviously a very important aspect of our December season!

the schloegles

It was almost noon when we heard the sound of hoofbeats and the jingle of harnesses. The sound carried forward just moments before the team of horses, sleigh and its occupants rounded the corner. At the first sign of the approaching visitors we rushed down onto the lake to await their arrival. And shortly the team of horses pulled up and came to an abrupt stop.

Frank Schloegle and his oldest boy, Louie, hopped off the sleigh. We shook hands all around and with the usual babbling banter that comes from not seeing anyone for a long period of time, these first pleasantries were a bit incoherent because everyone seemed to be speaking at once. With the general greetings out of the way, the horses needed to be looked after. The sleigh was heavy laden with fishing gear, camping gear, horse blankets and several bales of hay. After the horses were wiped down and blankets draped over them to ward off the chill, they were given a bit of hay to munch and were quite content. Horses taken care of, it was up to the cabin for tea and lunch.

With the advance knowledge of our visitors, Mum and Dad

had prepared a special meal. As we sat at the table filling our bellies with fresh fried moose meat, mashed potatoes and gravy, we got caught up on the current news. Freshly baked buns with sweet cranberry sauce were the finishing touches to a great meal. One more cup of tea and it was time for them to leave so they could get their own camp ready before nightfall. We watched them until they disappeared around the far northeast point. For some time we could hear the *clickety-clop* of the horses plodding along, the sound travelling across the ice and eventually subsiding. Dad would stop in and see them when he made his north run on Big Mahigan.

Meanwhile, it was time to set out the beaver lodge just north of the cabin. Dad had been saving this one; it was close and easy to check for quick Christmas money. One thing we'd noticed since the snow had fallen was the amount of muskrat "pushups" popping out of the snow along the shallower parts of the lake. The dark mounds protruded through the snow as the muskrats created their winter feeding stations. Clarence and I tagged along with Dad to watch him set out the beaver lodge. You had to be careful when you walked around the front of the lodge because the ice was considerably thinner where the beavers had their run and the ice was kept thin in this area due to the beavers' activity beneath the ice.

Several things kept their underwater runs free and clear: the air bubbles that followed the beavers when they left their platform inside and the air they expelled as they swam along. Movement was another factor; their swimming created a current and helped keep the ice from getting thick and preventing them from getting out. In general, there's usually more than one run per lodge: one they use for getting food and another as a return to bring it back. Once they nibbled the bark off a branch it was taken out and deposited beyond the feeding area and away from the lodge.

It's relatively easy finding these runs, especially early on in the season. A small scoop shovel was used to clear away the snow around the front edge of the lodge. After the snow was removed you could see where the air bubbles had accumulated. Once the run was established, a hole was chiselled through and the floating ice removed. *Wag-a-hoe* is the Cree name for a curved stick. The wag-a-hoe was used to feel the sides of the entrance under the ice. Then a short, dry pole of sufficient length was placed to stand vertical in the centre of the run. To this pole snares were attached, the number varying depending on the depth of the water. The lodge near us wasn't difficult and it didn't take us long to set out.

With ample time left in the afternoon a number of muskrat sets were made as well. We would concentrate on the push-ups and make an effort to trap some before the cold froze them out. Muskrat trapping is mainly geared for the spring season, but with the bountiful muskrats in the area they would be a good addition to our now-accumulating fur.

After setting all the traps we carried, there was still enough daylight to check the net. The pull generated a small amount of fish, which was just fine as this gave us a steady supply and enough fresh fish to eat. We closed off our day with a meal of rice, fresh fish and the homemade buns, whose fragrance still lingered in the cabin.

After a good night's rest, Dad readied himself for his regular northern run on Big Mahigan. He left long before sunrise. Now that things were back to a normal pace we had some time to concentrate on our own activities. Mum did her homemaking duties to get the cabin in order. I often wondered how it was that the place continually needed to be re-organized and cleaned, but I suppose my brother and I contributed to that need on a daily basis. Nevertheless, Mum seemed to have a steady and on-going task in homemaking.

Today was also bath day. The water pail had been set on the drum stove early on to heat. The bathtub was the same one used for scrubbing clothes. It was a very small, square galvanized tub and fortunately, we were still small enough to be able to bathe in it. One thing was for sure—once you were in, there wasn't much room for water, which was certainly a good way to conserve it! How much cleaner we were, I'm not sure, but it sure felt good—except for those few moments when you left the warm water before wrapping up in a warm towel and making a mad dash to stand beside the roaring fire. It didn't seem to matter how much we warmed the place, it always felt cold coming out of the tub. As usual, we started horsing around and as I bent over, the cheek of my bum touched the hot stove and *sssssst!*

"Ouch!" I screeched. Luckily it wasn't serious, although it *was* embarrassing. It did stop us from horsing around, though Clarence was the first to claim he'd had nothing to do with it and somehow found it real funny. Anyway, now that both her boys were clean behind the ears, Mum was able to get on with the rest of the household duties.

Only after we were good and dry did we tend to our own duties. We took water pails in hand and after several trips the water barrel was refilled, then the same for the wood box—several trips to the woodpile were needed to replenish the fast-dwindling firewood. As the chores wound down our attention returned to our own agendas. Mine was the constant battle of eliminating the mouse problem. I had given up on the small snares, having had absolutely no success with them. However, I now had modern-day technology! Dad had found a couple of mousetraps in the shack-tent. With renewed interest and a fresh sense of ambition I set the traps along the back wall of the cabin. And so, full of youthful confidence, I waited for the results of the harvest.

Mid-afternoon came and the cabin was quiet. Mum had settled into a peaceful battle with the never-ending jigsaw puzzle; the massive pile of pieces had grown less as the picture materialized. Her strategy was to tie-in the outer perimeter first and then work at filling in the rest. The fewer pieces there were, the faster the picture formed and we could tell Mum was getting anxious to see the finished product.

Suddenly, there was a snap in the far back corner of the cabin. What was it? It took just a moment to realize the mousetrap had been sprung into action. I went to check the results. Sure enough, a mouse! What a proud moment. Then I had a brain wave and thought it might be good to skin it out like a muskrat and stretch it. I wasn't sure what it could be used for, but what are ideas for? They're meant to be tried, surely? With this thought a small stretcher was carved and so began the painstaking chore of removing the tiny pelt the way Dad did with his furs. This took me a while to do, but I finally accomplished it and managed to get the tiny pelt stretched. I was real proud of the whole exercise.

We heard the sound of a team of horses and rushed over to look out the window just in time to see them pull up. Frank and Dad got off the sleigh and came in for hot coffee, their conversation wrapped around the day's events. After Dad left in the morning to check the trapline along the north shore of Big Mahigan, he had returned to the narrows where he met up with Frank and Louie. They'd set up their camp in a large stand of thick spruce trees on the northeast side of the narrows. This would be their base for commercial fishing the big lake. After a short visit, Frank and Louie offered to help Dad bring in the remainder of the moose meat. It didn't take long for the three of them and their team of horses to bring the whole load of meat across. It sure beat walking and dragging it back piece by piece. They'd dropped Louie off back at their camp when they passed through and after a short visit, which included lunch and coffee, Frank left.

The meat was hung up on the meat pole and covered with a tarpaulin. It had turned cold now and there were no more bears, so we only had to keep it from the ravens. A front shoulder was brought in to thaw out and hung up alongside the rest of the fur that needed defrosting.

There was time enough for a quick jaunt to check the muskrat sets nearby. It would be a late night for Dad since the catch was good today and there were a number of muskrats, beavers and squirrels to skin, flush and stretch, along with the fur previously thawed. Beavers were stretched mostly round (a bit towards oval being the proper shape) across a piece of plywood skin-side out, fastened with small nails at the outside edge and left to dry. There was room for two beaver pelts per stretcher, one on each side.

By now the cabin was filling up with an assortment of thawing fur, thawing moose meat, drying fur, the aroma of fresh-baked bannock and stew on the stove mixed with the added flavour of cigarette and woodsmoke. Accustomed to the lifestyle of a trapper, our acquired sense of smell adapted nicely to this combined fragrance for we were familiar with it, but at this point, the smell was probably intolerable to anyone else! "Trapper's perfume," as the saying goes. Regardless, when things slowed down it was Mum who bore the bulk of the continual struggle to sanitize the place. There were always a few days of moderate balance between the extremes of fur drying, heavy cooking and the powerful, clean smell of soap and bleach. And this was a period of high aroma—and not of clean soap and bleach, to be sure!

The next few days were hectic, maintaining the trapline and getting everything in order and up-to-date for the first trip into town with the fur. Frank and Louie had already made several trips into Big River with their fish at regular intervals, every second day. The fish were transported by horse team to the Schloegles' home and then by vehicle into Waite Fisheries, a fish processing plant in Big River. When the ice was thick and safe enough, they'd use a truck to haul the fish directly from the Mahigan portage. This opportunity for a ride into town would only last for a few days until the fish quota was reached. A commercially fished lake is gazetted for a set limit of pounds. The limit on Big Mahigan could be taken in a couple of weeks should the nets be in the right place at the right time.

Excitement was in the air! There were last-minute suggestions and items marked down on the long list of things to buy. Everything was caught up on the trapline and it would be fine for a few days if need be, especially if it turned cold since animals caught on the trapline would quickly freeze. It was decided that Mum and we boys would stay behind and hold the fort, while Dad went in alone to sell off the fur and buy the necessary staples to restock our bare cupboards. He would catch a ride in with the fish haul tomorrow.

We drifted off to sleep listening to Christmas tunes playing on the radio. And somewhere in the peaceful caverns of the mind just before sleep came "Silent Night, Holy Night, All is Calm, All is Bright."

the list

By the time daylight crested the snow-covered hills, all the fur had been packed into bundles—even my small package of mouse—then tied together and placed inside a tarpaulin for safe travel. The list was safely tucked away inside Dad's parka. There was always one section on the main list where a few personal items were marked down, and just to tease her a bit, I'll tell you that Mum's personal list went something like this: *new hairbrush, eyebrow pencil (brown), magazines (romance, you know the ones), puzzle (1500 pc.).* No matter how long this personal list was, the very last item on the list was always *cigs (Rothmans).* And to make sure there was no misunderstanding, she would always follow it up by adding *Rothmans.*

Our list was easy: *candy, pop, chocolate bar!*

We watched the team of horses as they slowly plodded across the frozen lake. Billowing clouds of white fog came from their nostrils as they exhaled warm air out into the freezing cold until they finally pulled up in front of the cabin and came to a halt. The three men gathered our cargo quickly into the sleigh and secured the rolled-up tarp next to the tubs of fish. Frank muttered a low command, "*Hie-yuh*, Queenie, let's go!" And with a flick of the reigns and a final wave, they were off. Dad figured he would be gone for a couple of days, which would allow him enough time to sell the fur, purchase the required goods and be back with Frank on his return.

We didn't linger outside long before the cold forced us back in. The chores were all done so we just stayed inside, enjoying the warmth of the cabin. The rest of the day went by extremely fast. Mum was enjoying her puzzle, which was down to just a few missing pieces. After awhile, Clarence and I finally had enough of the cabin and decided to brave the outdoors and go sliding. It had snowed a little more over the past few weeks and the trail we had carved down the hill became a great slide. In fact, we could almost make it to the woodpile behind the cabin! This time of year daylight was very stingy and it got dark early, so when the sun went down we went back inside to continue our horsing around, which Mum put a stop to right away.

For the evening meal, Mum had baked fresh bannock and fried thinly sliced moose meat. Fresh potatoes (long since gone) were replaced by a small batch of instant mashed. By the time we'd finished eating and supper dishes were put away it was time to listen to the "Northern News." And then bed.

We woke to the sound of Mum filling the heater with wood. It was really cold inside the cabin; we could see our breath, which made it even harder to leave the warm confines of the bedroll, but alas nature's call quickly overrode any hesitation and became a priority. It took a while to warm the place, even with a roaring fire, and the damper was set at its highest capacity, gauged by the appearance of the rising thermometer: how high the cherry red rose up the stovepipes safely. Even the barrel stove had red cheeks this morning. Eventually the heat won and pushed back the cold. Once it warmed up in the cabin, Mum cooked breakfast but first she had to chip ice off the top of the water bucket, a sure sign the temperature had really dropped. We were basically down to porridge now, and that heavily rationed. Powdered milk, sugar and many other dry ingredients were almost nonexistent. What was left we used sparingly. We were *so* looking forward to Dad's return!

We waited until mid-afternoon when the sun was at its highest before venturing out; there were a few rabbit snares to check. Bundled up in heavy winter gear we stepped out into the cold, frigid air. And was it ever cold! It just about took our breath away and each footstep squeaked on the hard, frozen surface of the snow. It was a good thing we only had a short distance to travel or we would have had to postpone the exercise. Still, it was worth going; the snares had captured a couple of rabbits. After resetting the snares, we made the short journey back. By the time we arrived at the doorstep our cheeks stung, frostbite nipping at our skin. The rabbits were hung inside to thaw for the evening meal. While we were still dressed, we topped up the water barrel and the woodbox. The cold snap meant there were four inches of ice to chisel through to get at the water.

There is something pristine about this type of cold. When the mercury wants to bust itself out from the bottom of a thermometer it's like a hush falls over the land. Everything huddles up and ceases to move, protection against the bone-chilling temperatures. Yet as the sun rises there are always a hardy few that venture out and take part in the day's affairs.

When the temperature plunged here, we didn't get the winds

and storms associated with the frigid Arctic barrens farther north, though the air turned crisp and biting and every sound was magnified. We could hear great distances through the dense cold. Multitudes of magnificent micro-crystals of frost glistened as they floated along—suspended, frozen in time—little flashes of light reflecting the sun's rays, pinpricks of white against the quiet serenity of the vast number of trees that formed the boreal forests of the region.

The day was coming to a close and it looked like another cold night. Hopefully it would warm up some by tomorrow; it wouldn't be at all pleasant for travelling if this extreme cold continued. We could feel the pressure from the cold outside as it tried to force itself in and met its match in the steady radiant heat of the stove, the warring factions most noticeable on the battleground of the thin plate glass of the cabin windows. We sat at the kitchen table eating our supper, watching each advance and retreat on the window panes as commanded by the convection of the air currents within the cabin: the tops dry but crusted with Jack Frost's brilliant designs sketched out in perfect, undulating contours; the middle sections slowly becoming damp until the moisture pooled enough that water droplets formed, these then running down towards the bottoms of the windows where it was cold enough to freeze solid and build up a blockade of ice. Mum would wipe the windows down with a towel and sop up any loose water and it would start all over again.

There was a message on the radio for us: "This is going out to Flora and the boys at Mahigan Lake. 'Will be arriving there about noon tomorrow.' This message is coming from Jim."

Now, that was great news! Clarence and I were making so much noise Mum had a hard time listening to the rest of the news. Our enthusiasm was short-lived—as if there weren't enough excitement, there was a knock on the door. Again reacting immediately, Clarence and I made a mad dash for our secret hiding spots and dead silence ensued. We peered out from behind our curtains, wondering who it could be. Mum answered the door and greeted the visitor—George! We scrambled out from our beds to welcome him. George explained he had met Dad and the Schleogles in the portage, and Dad had asked if he would swing by and check on us. We hadn't seen him for quite awhile and it was nice of him to come over.

The radio weatherman predicted an end to the Arctic front pushing its way through our region and the next few days' forecast looked hopeful, indicating moderate winter conditions. This was always good news—everything was made just a little bit easier and took a whole lot less energy. Speaking of energy, the gas lantern was out of fuel, we had run out of oil for the lamp and the last of the candles was gone. After these amenities were depleted, Mum used sardine cans filled with bear fat and a short length of cotton twine as a wick. We called this type of candle a bitch light, I'm not sure why. Regardless, with a few of these around the room there was plenty enough light to see by.

We were all at the table listening as George told us about the fur he'd caught and his plans to go in at Christmastime, which was soon. He was hoping for a bit more fur and wasn't sure whether he'd be able to snag a ride in with Frank. He figured the commercial fishing would be finished before he was ready to go out. In between mouthfuls of rabbit stew and bannock George brought us up to date with all his activities and current events—a good number of them seemed to be stretching the truth more than a little; George was always a great one for telling "the-big-one-that-got-away" tales. He was almost ready to go when we heard wolves howling; they sounded close.

Looking out the windows we could see dark figures running about the middle of the lake. At least a dozen wolves milled around the area where the bear carcass had been frozen in, though they had yet to approach the bait. They continued to investigate the area, advancing slowly as they determined whether or not it was safe to approach. We blew out all the lights in the cabin so we could see more clearly and waited for the moon to rise higher, watching from front row seats as the drama unfolded before us.

Some wolves ran in circles, some chased each other, some sat on their haunches and let loose the odd howl while others nosed around the ice. Wolves have an amazing sense of smell and can detect the smallest odour at great distances—even a bear carcass frozen under the ice and snow out in the middle of the lake can't remain hidden for long.

With the moonrise, the scene grew clearer. The wolves completed their inspection and closed in on the remains. When the moon was at its peak, George took action. Using Dad's rifle he slowly made his way outside and down towards the lake. His progress was slow and it took some time before he arrived at the spot he'd chosen for a firing position. We saw him line up the rifle, aiming in the direction of the wolves and then, after what seemed like a very long time, the report from the gun as George fired a shot, quickly followed by another and then a repeated *blam! blam! blam!*

The thunderous explosion of gunpowder sent the wolves off at a dead run in every direction, uncertain where to go because of the echoing rifle blasts. The sound bouncing back off the trees along the whole perimeter of the lake caused enough confusion to slow their retreat, giving George time to re-aim.

Blam! blam! blam!

Then it was quiet. The rifle had a ten-shot clip and as the silence grew we figured George had blasted his way through the whole thing, though a few wolves were still visible out on the lake.

Mum relit the bitch lights as George came back to the cabin. He had fired all the ammunition and at this point it looked like every shot had missed. We'd have to wait for daylight to find out for sure. George stayed awhile longer, watching to see if there was anything further, but after that episode it was a good guess that everything for miles around would keep still.

At any rate, George headed back to his cabin and we finally got to bed. The last sound we heard before sleep claimed us was the crinkling of the stovepipes as they expanded and contracted in the diminishing heat of the stove.

groceries

Morning dawned crisp and cold, but nothing like the forty-plus below the previous day had dealt us. In fact, because it had warmed up twenty degrees it actually felt quite nice. There was no wind, for which we were grateful. Although twenty below zero is still mighty cold, you can be comfortable providing you dress appropriate and stay dry.

It was still at least an hour away from the time we expected Dad to arrive, yet we were already taking turns outside, listening for any sound that might suggest they could be early. There was always the possibility of some incident slowing them down, but not today. They were right on schedule and by the time they rounded the final point we were standing on the ice—the wait and greet party. Certainly our smiles were broad enough!

It didn't take long to unload with all of us helping and soon the final box was taken off the sleigh. With the cold of the last two days Frank decided not to tarry any longer and left for his camp. When it was this cold out there was always the chance a net might freeze in. Frank would check them first and make sure the floats hadn't risen to freeze against the underside of the ice. With a wave they were off.

As we carried up the goods to the cabin, Dad told us briefly he'd received a decent price for the fur and there was even money left over. We told him of the events of the night before, and Dad said he'd go out later to have a look and see if there was any sign that a wolf had been hit. Hopefully there would be something to show for all the spent ammunition.

Now that everything was inside, we had fun taking items from their respective boxes—each a surprise package. It was kind of like opening Christmas presents. We sure appreciated having Frank freight in our goods. Dad was able to bring a lot more in and, with proper wrapping, even vegetables survived the trip unfrozen. And so, slowly getting buried in the midst of cardboard boxes and paper bags from the Red & White store, we boys helped take out the goods. Every time we came across something sweet there was a loud exclamation. There were a lot of groceries, including the personal items requested, but we didn't see any sign of presents—of any sort.

We *did* find the Eaton's catalogue. The Eaton's catalogue was our Christmas wish book, and we would completely devour the toy section, even using it to create imaginary storylines when we played, giving us hours of endless entertainment and satisfaction. It was a great book for peace of mind too, for it spared Mum and Dad countless hours of unnecessary noise, I'm sure. However, we weren't alone: we'd see Mum perusing the clothing and beauty section, and find Dad exploring the tools and hardware. It was a book for all of us and it met our needs in more ways than one, for when we ran out of toilet paper the wish book came in handy and a standing joke upon return from the outhouse was to say, "Oh, I just read a few pages—how much did *you* read today?"

Packed in among the groceries was a box of Japanese oranges, the fruit individually wrapped in lime green tissue paper. And, like the paper bags and boxes, everything was saved. Mum used these individual paper wraps for decorations, but we thought their best use was for something more along the lines of the catalogue during an emergency!

Once things were sorted, we went about the rest of the day's affairs. The net was checked, pulling in a few fish for that night's supper. There were also store-bought jam tarts for dessert and we were looking forward to that.

Mum was really pleased not to have to smoke handmade rollies now that she had her Rothmans cigarettes. She was further thrilled to find a new puzzle to challenge her. The previous one had been finished, although it was missing a piece. We never really heard Mum swear much—profanity wasn't really in her vocabulary—but when she discovered a puzzle piece was missing, we did hear, "Shit!" Now, I can't say for sure whether we had anything to do with that missing piece or not, but Mum solved it by making up the missing link with a piece of cardboard. With the large cardboard boxes we now had she could make a base and glue the puzzle down with a mixture of flour and water. A new comb and a restocked supply of romance magazines and she was all set for a good portion of the winter. With her personal stuff stored safely away, the small task of folding the paper bags and boxes for future use became a priority to restore enough room to move around the cabin.

After the fish were brought in, Dad went to check the line along the spring. Meanwhile, Mum started preparing the evening meal. She was really excited. It had been a while since we'd had all the ingredients to make a full-course meal.

As nightfall gradually erased the remaining light, the activities of the day wound down. On Dad's return from checking the closest run, he veered by the bear carcass. There were certainly a lot of wolf tracks, but nothing to show that George had done any damage. Mum had the supper table set and ready when Dad got back and we sat down to the long-awaited supper. We were not disappointed and the wait was worth every minute. Fresh-caught whitefish, fresh mashed potatoes with canned cream and butter, cream-style corn and deep-browned pork and beans. There was almost not enough room to fit in the jam tarts! But tough as it was, we found the room.

As the evening came to a close, Clarence and I pored over the toy section of the catalogue, preparing mental notes of what we wanted Santa to bring us when he came down from the North Pole, and hoping he wouldn't forget us, being way out in the wilderness and such. Mum and Dad went through the mail that had accumulated in town over the past few months. There were the usual reminders of accounts due, but most of them knew we were seasonal. Letters from Grandma, both for us and for Mum as well. Grandma always sent a dollar bill and even though it was nice to receive her card, it was also nice to dream of how we were going to spend the money when we got to town. That dollar neatly tucked into her Christmas card was a blessing to us and Grandma continued this tradition well into our teens, though the dollar increased to a fiver then!

Dad mentioned he'd showed the fur buyer my stretched mouse and the guy must've had the Christmas spirit because he gave me two bits or twenty-five cents for it, which was a lot of money. It would buy a bottle of Coke and a chocolate bar at the Red & White store in Big River, although it would burn a hole in my pocket for a long time before I'd be able to spend it because it would be several months before any of us would go in again. With the evening well on and a mindful of interests mined from the wish book, we finally succumbed to the sandman.

When morning came we found that Dad was long gone. He'd left well before sunrise to check the line towards the north but left us with instructions to go out and collect a Christmas tree as part of our chores for the day. We didn't mind the addition of this extra task at all. In fact, we decided to go and do this all-important job first thing, before Mum in a real strict tone of voice reminded us of our jobs in sequential importance: "Wood and water, first thing!" We didn't wait to be told twice and made short work of hauling in the wood and bringing in the water.

Clarence, being older than me, was always conjuring something up. Him and all his neat ideas! I don't know why I always had to be part of his experiments, though. For whatever reason, he chose that moment to discuss the laws of gravity with me and told me that if you swung a pail in a circle, the force of the rotation would keep the water from spilling. It sounded just fine to my way of thinking—so long as he tried it first. So, with his pail half full of water he started the process by swinging the bucket back and forth a few times until there was enough momentum, and then with a final swing, around it went, *whoosh!* Sure enough, it worked! Now it was my turn. I followed his technique exactly and with a final swing, around it went, *whoosh!* Trouble was, the *whoosh* went out of it halfway up and the pail and its contents poured out all over me! The bright side of this was that Clarence had to finish the rest of the chores himself!

It took a while for Mum to calm me down and get me dried off but eventually she succeeded and I was ready for the next challenge. We didn't have to go far to get a nice Christmas tree. There were several just beyond the perimeter of our cleared site. Small Swede saw in hand we wandered around some of the shorter spruce trees until we spotted one that stood out from all the rest. It was about five feet high with uniform thick, deep green boughs. Clarence told me to hold it while he cut it, but my abilities at this age were limited and most tasks seemed monumental, especially those involving my brother. As soon as the tree had been sawn through, Clarence stepped back and yelled, "Tim-berrr!" and watched the small tree fall over. After he dug me out of the snow and saw I was all right he bust a gut. I just couldn't see any humour in it whatsoever, but we did work together and manage to tow the tree back to the cabin without any further incident.

While we were still outside I pulled up my small trapline. Empty. I decided to call it quits. A small weasel had made the space underneath of the cabin its home and they are a hundred times better than a cat when it comes to catching mice. A weasel is a ferocious animal and soon clears out any local mice, so thus ended my trapping season.

Mum had a stand to set the tree in. Once it was secure we wanted to get down to the business of making ornaments for it, but Mum wanted to let it thaw out first before we attached anything. Hindsight suggests she was waiting for Dad.

It was close to nightfall when he arrived home. As soon as he came in, he said, "I see you boys dragged in the tree." We didn't know if it was a question or a statement, but we both responded with a proud "Yup!" then proceeded to tell him all about it, but

Dad cut us off, "I can tell that you dragged it in backwards by all the spruce boughs you left on the trail." After giving the tree the once-over, Dad muttered, "It's amazing there's anything left on it at all!" However, the fact that his packsack was full of fur and that we'd all had real good day helped everyone see the humour in it and the tree stayed. It was time for supper and then we'd decorate the tree. And so the tree-hunting job was given to us boys, and for many years after we continued the tradition of picking out all sorts of varieties in different shapes and sizes.

After supper, Mum popped corn to thread on a string for garland. Clarence and I helped out by eating the loose popcorn and unwrapping the green tissue paper squares from around the Japanese oranges. We ate a few oranges as we went along, just loving them because they were so easy to peel. They were a real treat and marked the holiday season proper, since we could only get this type of orange during the pre-Christmas season. Mum put a stop to us eating any more, though, not just to save the oranges, but to keep us from getting the runs!

And with that, it was bedtime. Tomorrow was another day and the tree could be finished then.

christmas

Over the next few days work filled our waking hours. The shorter days didn't allow much time to get everything done and it was a mad dash to complete our chores. The long evenings were actually enjoyable, provided there was something to do—which never seemed to be a problem because something always cropped up and needed attention.

The decorating of the tree was an ongoing process. We did most of it right away, but extra ornaments were added until it had been nicely decorated. Many of the decorations were cut-out cardboard figures and designs wrapped in tinfoil and attached to the tree by small loops of strong thread. Because Mum stayed in camp she didn't have the opportunity to buy a Christmas present for Dad, but while he was away on a run, she hand-stitched a gift for him, ready just in time for the big day.

As the commercial fishing wound down, we were fortunate to get in the last-minute staples that would supply our needs comfortably until early spring. On their last trip out, Frank and Louie stopped in for a quick visit. The fishing had gone extremely well and they reached the limit without any trouble. Frank told us he'd be back in early spring and would let us know when. He was in Big River regularly and if there was something of importance for us he'd let us know over "Northern News," otherwise he would bring it in the spring. After a short visit we said our goodbyes, and with the usual "Merry Christmas!" and "Happy New Year!" they were off.

After the Schloegles left, things quieted down and the next few days were spent in the normal routine of everyday life on a trapline, with the small exception of the impending visit of the man in red, riding a sleigh pulled by reindeer. And then!

'Twas the night before Christmas and all was silent…right! Not so for two eager boys who didn't know *patience* was actually a word meant to slow down time. On Christmas Eve we had a special evening meal. Mum and Dad helped each other make this Christmas banquet. There was a nice leg of ham roasted to perfection and sliced into controllable pieces and mashed potatoes whipped with real cream until they formed brilliant white peaks. Dad made a special white sauce with fresh green peas, a recipe that his mum, Florence, used on occasion, and as far as Dad was concerned it was the best in the world.

GRANDMA FLORENCE'S WHITE SAUCE WITH PEAS

2 tbsp melted butter
2 tbsp flour (sifted)
¼ tsp salt
1 cup milk (cream)
1 cup peas

Mix butter and flour, then gradually add milk, stirring quickly. Bring to a boil and then reduce heat, adding the salt. Cook a bit longer (about a minute) always stirring. Fold in steamed peas.

Mum baked fresh homemade bread and the leftover dough went into a cinnamon roll. There was fresh apple pie as well. It had been burning a hole through the shelf it sat on ever since it was put there to cool. Knowing we would be having a large scoop of French vanilla ice cream with it was just about too much for us to bear. What a tremendous meal, and again there was almost not enough room for the pie—almost!

Suddenly, Dad perked up and said, "Did you hear that?" Of course, we hadn't. And then he said, "There it is again, a noise! Did you hear it?" By this time I think Clarence and I were about ready to lift off. He suggested we go and hide and we didn't have to be told twice; I don't think our feet hit the floor from the kitchen table to our hideaway beneath our bed.

Thoughts of ghosts past from that Indian village Mum had talked about flitted through my mind, but Clarence had his own imagination going, his emotions running high with excitement as he thought for sure Eaton's had delivered the whole catalogue! Either way, fear or excitement, we were about ready to explode.

Dad told us he was going out to see what had made the noise and we were to remain quiet. That was no problem for me, but Mum literally had to sit on Clarence to hold him down.

Soon we heard Dad return.

And lo and behold, there were presents under the tree, all gift-wrapped! Dad explained that Santa had had to stop off early and had apologised that he couldn't wait for us to fall sleep. We didn't mind! Now came a true understanding of that new word added to our vocabulary: patience!

When we were finally released it was like the first storm of the season; there was gift wrap flying in every direction! Somewhere in the background we could hear Mum telling us to try and save the paper, but to no avail. Our tradition now is to open one gift Christmas Eve and the rest in the morning, but maybe because we were still little we dove right into them that year and opened them early, even though it seemed like it took all night. Mum and Dad sat at the table sharing their gifts while we got buried in ours. There were the general, useful gifts of socks and mitts and a new toque—even a package of several boys' briefs. And then there were the toys! We got games like Chinese Checkers and Snakes-n-Ladders. There were toy soldiers, a barrel of monkeys, pick-up sticks and something that was stacked and you pulled out pieces until it came crashing down.

And there were a few solitary toys for personal enjoyment, like dinky cars, planes and an assortment of tiny vehicles. Then Dad mentioned that something had been left outside and we would see it the next day. While we were completely engrossed, Mum and Dad opened their gifts. They each had a number of new clothing items that were not wrapped, but the special gift for Dad was gift-wrapped with a fancy bow. Mum had stitched together a beautiful pair of moosehide gauntlets with beaver trim. This type of leather mitt was a welcome gift for any trapper on cold winter days.

Mum had already received most of her gifts along with her personal stuff earlier, with the exception of one. Now she painstakingly removed each piece of scotch tape and with careful consideration took the wrapping off the gift, and we really thought it was going to take all night. I think Dad was on the edge of learning the meaning of that new word *patience* as well. Finally, her gift was opened, revealing a paint-by-numbers kit. It had several numbered images and a whole lot of paint tubes. Mum was some happy!

And as if that wasn't enough, there came a sound from outside that even we boys heard. It came a second time and shortly after there was a knock at the door.

Again, Clarence and I grew wings and flew for cover! Dad opened the door and there was George, carrying a packsack and wearing a silly grin. Mum brought out the leftovers from supper and reheated a portion. Between mouthfuls, George dug into his bag and brought out a gift for Mum, a big box of assorted chocolates. For Dad he had brought a bottle of whiskey—this put a smile on Dad's face as he thoroughly enjoyed indulging in the festive season.

And for Clarence and me, he dug out of that Christmas bag two plastic toy machine guns that actually operated. When you pulled the trigger, it spun a counterweight that activated a flint, creating sparks that simulated gunfire. It even made machine gun sounds—*rat-at-tat-tat!*—with each squeeze of the trigger. It got pretty loud pretty quick in that one-room cabin with Clarence and me defending the nation in battle. And Mum, Dad and George, they were getting loud as well and seemed to be talking at the same time—must've been trying to hear each other over the racket we were making and, of course, it certainly couldn't have been the whiskey! At any rate, Dad finally decided it was bedtime and things quieted down then. Sleep came with dreams of the something still waiting outside.

The next morning was a bit quiet. George was long gone by then, though he had stayed over—no surprise as I imagine they celebrated long into the night. When we woke up, Dad already had the cabin warm, Mum had finished cleaning up the paper wrappings and both of them looked somewhat subdued. Clarence and I got up and had breakfast before we remembered whatever it was outside. Curious, we quickly put on our outdoor clothes and headed out to investigate.

There leaning against the cabin was one of those fancy wooden toboggans with the curl in front! It was about four feet in length with a small pull rope attached. In no time we were at the hill, and now we were able to make it all the way to the cabin—even past it a few times!

After we went back in we couldn't find the toy guns anywhere but as time went on we forgot about them. It was sometime later Mum told us that Dad had burned them in the barrel stove the night of the Christmas party because we had just about driven him nuts with all those *rat-at-tats*. Apparently sparks were flying from more than just the toy machine guns…!

The truly amazing fact about the whole evening was that George, after missing the last trip out with Frank, had then walked out with snowshoes through the portage and across Smoothstone Lake. From there he'd been able to catch a ride to sell off his furs in Big River. He quickly made the return journey and delivered the presents in time for Christmas Eve—a distance of almost fifty miles—all for a family living on the trapline. What a Christmas gift in itself!

Many years later I had the opportunity to publicly thank George for his unselfish act of kindness. George also recalled that Clarence and I were a little over the top that night too! But we still remember his thoughtfulness with a tremendous amount of gratitude. It is a memory to last a lifetime.

new year's

Christmas over, things slowed down some. On December 31, we stayed up until midnight, waiting to ring in the New Year and monitoring the radio for the final countdown as the host for the evening broadcast them.

"Five. Four. Three. Two. One...!"

The radio announcer went ballistic over the air and shouted something that we could only imagine was "Happy New Year!"

Dad went outside and fired off a few quick rounds with his faithful .303. At times like this he didn't mind wasting a few bullets. All of us gathered just outside the door, listening to the echoes recede to parts unknown. Suddenly the age-old tradition was repeated and we heard shots fired further down the lake where George was also ringing in the New Year. George obviously didn't mind blasting off a few celebratory rounds of his own as well.

After some brief whoops into the night air, we calmed down enough to listen for any other rifle reports, but there was nothing further. I'm sure that any wildlife near enough and possibly nature itself had questions about this type of behaviour from those they shared this country with. And so the New Year was rung in.

Our winter then settled into a regular routine of scheduled events that allowed the days to pass almost unconsciously. Sometimes daylight was nearly nonexistent; the sky heavily layered with a thick blanket of grey cloud cover. Yet other times we had almost six solid hours of good sunshine. There was a steady flow of fur coming in now and it wasn't very often Dad returned without something to pay for expenses and cover costs.

The odd blizzard caused a whiteout now and then, but they were never enough to put things on hold for more than the regular time we'd normally wait to check the line anyway. The snow flurries blew in short intervals and the snow itself slowly accumulated to an average of about two feet.

One of the greatest gifts Mother Nature offered us was weather that held pretty steady throughout the coldest months of winter. Oh, there were times when the temperature plummeted and we suffered a cold snap, but as a rule these didn't last long and in most cases it stayed between ten and twenty degrees below zero. It was a dry cold and as long as the winds weren't extreme it was quite bearable. The key to survival was to dress in layers; you could always add or remove articles of clothing as the need arose. Another very important aspect was to try your best not to get all sweated up, as this eliminated the insulating value of the clothing and made it unreliable for warmth.

When a blizzard did blow through we tended to curl up and stay close to the warmth of the stove. There was always something set aside for days like this. Mum had already started another one of her puzzles and worked on it occasionally, but her

Mum's paint-by-number picture of our home

main interest was the paint-by-number set she had gotten from Dad. She thoroughly enjoyed this pastime and it didn't take her long to complete the pictures. With the leftover paints she decided to paint a picture of our cabin. The only canvas available was cardboard from the boxes Dad had brought before Christmas. Nevertheless, she cut out a section and pencilled on her own sketch of our home. Once that was to her liking, she started painting small portions as time allowed. Clarence and I stayed out of the picture (and her hair!), having learned our lesson after the dilemma of the missing puzzle piece.

Dad had his own ideas of a hobby, though he did take short turns at the new puzzle as well. Mostly, though, Dad discussed ideas and evaluated what the cost would be for an aircraft of some sort, and then he would draw up a plan and see if it was worth the effort. In 1954, Dad had been out in British Columbia for several months and while he was there acquired a private pilot's licence at the Langley Prairie Airport in Langley, B.C. That was the spark of his desire to own his own plane. But for now, these were just ideas and after they had been exhausted, he stored them on a mental shelf for future deliberation.

Dad filled in the time by telling stories of past adventures. This was a favourite pastime for us too, since one of Dad's greatest attributes was his tremendous ability to share a story; he had the gifts of a true storyteller.

One blizzardy day we weren't going anywhere and had lots of time. So, despite the howling wind that made the frigid temperatures seem even colder, snug inside while a blinding snowstorm raged on, we settled down and burrowed deep into the warmth of our quilts and the safety of our cabin to listen to Dad's stories. And soon the heat and comfort of the cosy cabin enveloped us and we became drowsy. Eyelids heavy, it didn't take long before we were sound asleep, dreaming of the survival of the fittest.

anton mylengar

The storm brought several inches of snow with it, which would mean checking all the lines and raising the snares again. Dad gathered his trapping equipment and was off before the day dawned.

After our regular chores, we were to go and clean the snow and chisel out the net holes. It had become our job to check the net when Dad was busy on the line. The net continually produced small amounts of fish. Today there was a little more than usual since we had missed a day because of the blizzard, but it was nice to have the extra bit of fish and what we didn't eat fresh was taken out behind the cabin and stored in nature's deep freeze.

The frozen fish were preserved by dipping them several times in cold water until they were completely sealed in a thin coating of ice. Glazing the fish in this manner helped keep the tender meat fresh and prevented freezer burn. When there were enough Mum ground them up and made them into fish patties. Clarence and I always looked forward to these patties and appreciated them as a treat, something out of the ordinary and a real delicacy.

Once the chores were done there was time to blast down the hill on the new toboggan. Clarence figured out a way to get a lot more speed out of our downhill plunge. He'd stuff me in front of the toboggan at the top of the hill and make me wait. Oh, it was like the calm before the storm! Then, at a dead run, he'd attack from behind, literally shoving me head first into the curl at the front end of the toboggan. I would careen downhill like I was in an Olympic bob-sled race with Clarence at a full gallop alongside, and about the time me and the toboggan grew wings, he would hop in behind. Clarence was really pleased with the results of this massive effort because we gained about an extra four feet in the fresh snow—whoopee! I didn't share his enthusiasm at all because as we ploughed on through, most of that soft white stuff was funnelled down the full length of my back! After a few of these episodes I realized the fun factor wasn't going to improve any and called it quits for the day.

Clarence leaned the toboggan against the cabin wall and called out, "Dad!" as he pointed at the north end of the lake. We could see Dad rounding the far northeast point and it wasn't long before he arrived, heavily laden with fur. It was a good haul and he was thrilled to be bringing in a lynx, a large male cat with exceptional markings. Even though the lynx were at the top of their cycle, this particular area didn't suit them well and it wasn't often we caught one, even though we'd been seeing a lot of signs of them lately—more than usual due to the increase in their food supply—rabbits—which had become rather bountiful as they too reached the top of their cycle.

The following day came in nice and mild with a gorgeous

sunrise and a full blue sky, calm and peaceful. The only sound was a small flock of snow birds chirping happily as they made their way along the lake, feeding on fresh seeds fallen off a few of the smaller trees that dotted the shoreline. It was wonderful to watch these almost all-white snow birds fluttering about; by some unseen command they did everything in unison. The tiny bit of black on their heads and wingtips stood out against the blank sheet of snow. They darted in and out of view, foraging for the tiny tidbits spread across the surface of the snow.

Dad went across to check the short run along the spring section of the trapline. He wasn't gone very long since it was a short line and returned carrying on his back a wolf that had been snared in one of the sets along the small stream.

Once back home Dad immediately went to work skinning out the animal. Dad always had a problem with the smell of wolves and could only stand working on them a few minutes at a time, barfing out his guts in between sessions of removing the pelt. It wasn't really funny, but Clarence and I enjoyed the black humour of the whole affair. And we were never really sure whether it was the odour of the wolf or the Skoal snuff he so thoroughly enjoyed while on snowshoes that caused the problem, or a combination of both, perhaps. Dad was, however, able to complete the task and get it stretched. All in all, another great addition to the family income.

It was one of those days when you just couldn't stay inside. It was hardly past noon and we were standing outside looking at the fresh snowshoe tracks crossing the lake. There is always something melancholy about a snowshoe trail leading away and vanishing in the distance: its solitary serenity, the only marked path in the snow, leaves you with the question of what might be found out there.

This peace was short-lived, though, the silence broken by the sound of a motor from the south end of the lake. The rumble increased until we were sure someone was rounding the point when suddenly all became quiet. Soon after we heard voices in the still air—but then nothing again. A few moments passed and George came running along the shore, yelling for Dad to come and help him get a machine and sleigh out of a heavily slushed over area. He was a little out of breath as he explained that Anton had come with him and was still in the sleigh. He and Dad both took off down the lake at a run while we waited anxiously to find out what was happening.

Meanwhile, Mum rushed to the cabin to make sure there would be enough hot coffee ready for them when they returned. It was only a few minutes before the snowmobile drove up with Dad, George and a soaking wet Anton encased in a layer of snow and ice. At the moment he was plastered and still carrying a bottle of whisky. Dad and George almost had to cut him out of the sleigh. Once they removed his outer wrappings, they hauled him inside to thaw out. After a few cups of hot coffee were poured into him—during which he told everyone within earshot he detested them in no uncertain terms—Anton started to come around, but as soon as the combination of warmth and alcohol hit him, he fell asleep.

George explained that he had gone to Big River to sell off his fur and on his return had stayed over at Anton's. George was interested in the snowmobile and was planning to buy it. Anton suggested they do a test run and make a trip to the old stomping grounds to see "Yimmy," as he called Dad. This would give George a good idea of the machine's capabilities. But Anton liked his booze and wouldn't leave home without it, so while George drove there was a one-man party going on in the sleigh he was towing. By the time they were across Smoothstone and through the portage, the old man was on his second bottle. When George stopped to check on his companion, Anton was already completely hammered, but by that stage there was no other alternative than to carry on. Just before rounding the last point before reaching our cabin, they ran into deep slush. It was fortunate they were so close already, though Dad said that Anton would never have frozen anyway with the amount of antifreeze he had in him!

George had done well with his fur and told us he'd be buying the snowmobile. After polishing off the rest of Anton's bottle of whiskey, George left for his cabin and told us he'd be back for Sleeping Beauty before noon the following day, returning with the rest of his supplies.

And it wasn't long before Anton awoke and shared news of the outside world. He had been all the way out to Prince Albert on some sort of business we didn't quite understand, but while he was talking he brought out a few coils of coloured beads and an assortment of tanned hide for Mum. Anton had a real strong German accent, and mixed with being bushed, it was hard to make out his broken English. Dad had lived with Anton and known him for many years, so he had no trouble communicating with him. As Anton passed the gifts to Mum, he said, "Tack-em, Puh-low-ruh Yeen, Deese-er-fer-yuh." (*Take them, Flora Jean, these are for you*). Mum really appreciated this, knowing there was a strong bond of friendship with him because of her relationship with Dad. Of course, we boys received gifts as well, but mostly items that contributed to a terrible amount of tooth decay! We didn't mind. And last but not least, there was another bottle of his favourite brand of whiskey to share.

Dad, Mum and Anton celebrated far into the night and from what I could gather, it seemed there were a dozen different conversations taking place and not one on the same topic.

Clarence and I stayed awake, even after Mum and Dad went to bed. It seemed like Anton had an endless supply of drink and a bottomless pit to put it in as well. The strange thing about this whole episode was his reaction to the tunes playing on the radio. In the candlelight, he waved his hands over the radio and repeated over and over again, "Eye-duh-net-vork-she ees-a-yal-lin-me." (*Yes, the network is calling me*). Anton finally went and lay down on the foam mattress, but as the cabin cooled down he reached over and grabbed a small roll of insulation and snuggled into it. Now, there were three things that Anton hated most in life: one was rubber boots, which he called "rheumatism boots"—he'd only wear them in a dire emergency—and the second was insulation. As a rule just the thought alone would drive him up a wall. Well, guess what? When he woke up the next morning that expression, "the shit hit the fan" was the right one!

The third item on his hate list was water. After he came back in from rolling around in the snow and while he was still in shock, Mum gave him the washtub and a towel. It was the first time us boys saw Anton clean, shaved and sober!

So, it turned out to be a fine visit after all. George arrived just before noon and drove around the cabin, parking the snowmobile at the front entrance. Shortly after, we said our goodbyes and it was then you could tell that Mr. Mylengar had a real soft spot for his "Yimmy." We could see it in Dad as well.

Dad was to see Anton several times over the next few years, but this was the last trip Mr. Mylengar made into Mahigan. Clarence and I saw him only once more before his death. Anton had one brother, August. He stayed with Anton for a short time before he moved out West, but I don't recall ever meeting or seeing Anton's brother.

There's always a subdued feeling after visitors leave. It's a loss, in a sense: for a short while you share your surroundings with someone and then they're gone. Eventually the vacuum fills and the vacant space is gone, and you get on with your daily agenda and life at hand. After the sound of the snowmobile vanished there was time to check the net and a few sets along the northwest shore. And with that the day came to a quiet close.

chinook and philion lake

Only a few days after our guests had gone we all woke up to a change in the weather, a change in the pressure of the air. The wind gradually increased until there was a constant blow from over the west hill that remained steady and strong. As the daylight increased, so too did the temperature. The combination of sun and westerly wind was like heat radiating from a roaring fire in the old drum stove and soon the cold disappeared.

Dad was all excited and he yelled at us to get out of bed and get outside and feel how warm it was. Meanwhile, we were trying to rub the sleep out of our eyes and I was trying to avoid getting a swift kick from Clarence, who was more than a little sceptical about being woken so early despite the warm weather.

Dad explained that it was a chinook. On rare occasions, a warm westerly would blow in during the winter months and heat the air and land to the point of thaw. These chinooks only lasted a day or so but we tremendously enjoyed these reminders that spring was just around the corner.

Outside, the black-capped chickadee sang its merry tune of "spring's here, springs here." The small birds were fooled by the sudden change in weather, but hey! we forgave our small feathered friend; we were excited by the warmth too. The wind also carried another sound. At first there was a loud, muffled bang and then a sound similar to a chicken drumming up a date, although it was still too early for them as there was plenty of winter left. The sound floated across the airwaves for some time, *whirr, whirr, whirr* and then there was nothing but silence.

We were all curious.

By the next day, the warm chinook air had blown through and the winds had calmed down. The temperature dropped again but it was still very mild out. Taking advantage of this, Dad prepared to snowshoe into Philion Lake, with plans to keep a look-out for whatever had caused the unusual noise. Philion Lake was several miles to the south and known for its large amounts of muskrat and beaver. Dad had wanted to explore the lake for some time and the mild weather meant it was feasible to go in and check it out. With packsack and the necessary gear, he was gone before daylight. There was an old portage to the lake, but the broken part of the trail only went so far. George used it as part of his trapping area, although he didn't go into Philion itself, so Dad expected to break trail for some distance and told us he would be returning very late.

In the meantime, we still had our regular chores that needed attending and when daylight arrived we left to pull in the net. We had put some rough fish in a pile close to the where the net was fished and since our last check wolves had paid a visit to the area. They'd consumed every scrap of fish, leaving nothing behind—we weren't the only ones taking advantage of the chinook.

One good thing about the warm weather was that very little work was required to clear the ice from the hole. In fact, we didn't use the ice chisel at all—the shovel was sufficient to clean and trim the hole. After pulling the net back under the ice we loaded the few good fish and returned to camp where Mum cleaned and prepared them for the evening meal. Along with the fish, Mum was going to make bread, and as rule when she made bread there would also be a treat...possibly dough-gotts, or maybe even doughnuts. A little constructive whining might work.

Nightfall brought in a beautiful winter evening. It was clear and the temperature just below freezing with no wind. Mum had fried up the fish and along with them came rice and fresh buns. True to form, there was a treat too and it was extra special as it turned out to be cinnamon rolls—all that positive input paid off! While we were eating, a message came over the "Northern News" from Frank. He would be making a trip in to the fishing camp, bringing in a few supplies. We could expect him in a couple of weeks. This was great news because Mum and Dad had talked about going in to sell off the fur that had accumulated and now they could.

It must have been around midnight when Dad came in and it looked like he was ready to call it a day for sure. Mum shared the message about Frank coming while heating a plate of leftovers and pouring a hot cup of tea. Dad said he would tell us about his trip in the morning and with that it was bedtime—which was good since we could hardly keep our eyes open anyway.

When morning came we were up like a pair of jackrabbits—well, sort of! But we were interested in knowing what Dad had found out in Philion Lake country. Dad started by telling us he had followed George's trail, which had gone about two-thirds of the way before turning to some other area. From that point on he was breaking new trail. It was tough slogging as the snow was deep and powdery back in the hills. Still, it was an enjoyable walk and at one point he came across a meadow where several moose had bunched together. The area was covered in tracks and their beds were all over the place, shaped like huge white bowls frozen in the snow. The moose had been around this area for a while and they didn't seem afraid of human presence. Dad counted four animals slowly moving off into the bush on the far side of the meadow and he was almost certain there were just as many again that he couldn't see. Bulls have a tendency to group together over the winter and it's not a total surprise to come across more than a few animals in one location at the same time. Not much further along and on a higher piece of ground there was another moose. This was a cow already heavy in calf. Dad secretly hoped that the wolves would stay away from her; if they attacked, the cow moose would have no chance whatsoever. Yet there are always some that make it through this dangerous period of time.

After arriving at Philion, he circled the lake. First down one side until he could see the south shore clearly, then he cut directly across to the west shore and went back up again to meet his back-trail, watching out for the watershed because the lake drained out close to the northwest end. Philion River was small and it led out to Smoothstone a few miles to the west. Once he'd completed the circuit it was time to break for tea.

Using the snowshoes to pack down an area in which to build a fire took only a few moments; it almost looked like he was doing a jig—a snowshoe dance of sorts. The chosen spot had plenty of small dry growth close at hand, making it an easy task

Snowshoes set up as a windbreak

to gather enough wood to fuel the fire for a long while. Once the fire was going, he packed down the rest of the area in front of a large old spruce tree. The massive branches near the bottom stretched out for many feet, as if to out-do the ones above in reaching for the lake. After shaking the limbs hard enough to knock off the snow so it wouldn't fall into the fire, Dad trimmed a few branches to make a small, warm and inviting alcove. A willow was cut down, limbed and jammed into the snow at an angle to support the teapot, and snow scooped from underneath was better as it had started to crystallize and held more moisture. This was added to the teapot until there was enough water for a few cups of tea.

It proved to be a great place to sit back and have lunch. The base of the tree had one large limb protruding out near the bottom, and after trimming it with the axe it made a perfect place to sit. The snowshoes were taken off, the ends shoved into the snow beside him tail first to be used as a temporary coat hanger for Dad's outer parka. With the water at a boil and a teabag thrown in, Dad soon found a small stick with a bit of a hook in it to use to remove the kettle from the fire and set aside to steep. Making tea this way allowed its flavour to be enhanced by the smoke of the campfire. Trappers often talk about their experiences in the wilderness and many times campfire tea is included in the conversation. Bannock warmed on the red hot coals along with a few pieces of sliced roast moose made up the rest of the meal.

Sitting there with your back to the tree, campfire radiating heat, a terrific view of the lake against the deep blue sky and a crystal clear winters' day—you just couldn't ask for anything better. We could picture the place as Dad talked.

Meanwhile, mesmerized by this tranquil solitude and relishing the buttered bannock dipped into his cup of sugar-sweetened tea, time seemed to stand still. Then something caught Dad's attention. There was movement along the west shoreline, about a third of the way down the lake. A large, black timber wolf soon revealed itself, the massive creature emerging from the tall reeds and bulrushes prevalent along these shorelines.

The wolf made a beeline across the lake, stopping only to investigate Dad's snowshoe tracks. After a few moments of sniffing out the trail, it continued on across with a slow lope, again stopping at the snowshoe trail on the opposite side of the lake. A quick sniff determined that the scent was older than the one it had previously come across and the wolf carried on its easterly journey. With one last look aimed directly at Dad's campsite, as if to say, "I know you're there," it moved into the tall grass and vanished. With that, it was time to finish the tea and put the gear back in the packsack.

The sun was already going behind the tall trees to the west and casting long shadows, suggesting it was high time to get back on the trail. Even though there was a fair amount of daylight yet, once in the thick of the forest it would darken considerably and night would come fast. However, there was a good back-trail to follow and once George's trail was reached there would be no problem getting home, although it would be late.

Snowshoes laced and packsack on, Dad was off for home and family, hoping the moonlight would brighten the way. As it turned out, it was a great trip back; the weather remained mild—just cold enough to make walking pleasant and not build up a heavy head of steam—and when the moon did come out it was enough to see the trail. Times like this are precious and rare. Dad felt pure joy in the sound the snowshoes made with each passing step, the *swish-swish, swish-swish* and gentle creak of the lacings as they tightened and loosened with each swinging arc. All of this was like a song mixed yet in tune with his thoughts, then suddenly, there was the cabin and the welcome-home candle placed at the window.

After Dad shared his adventure, it was time to go out on the line. Because he was so sore from yesterday's long trek he chose to do the short run at the spring. Clarence and I finished our own chores then went to check a few rabbit snares nearby. Mum had told us to get out of her hair for awhile, and we didn't ask why either. It was so nice out we took advantage of it and played trapper, hunter and a super hero of some sort, all at the same time. The first few rabbit snares produced nothing, but in the last few sets we achieved our goal and came home bearing the fruits of our labour. We were almost at the door when we heard a couple of reports from a rifle in the direction of the spring and, curious, waited outside to see what it was all about. We watched as Dad made his way across and when he walked up he wore a silly grin bordering on sheepishness. Now we were *really* interested and followed him inside, literally stepping on his heels. Over a cup of tea he explained the shots we'd heard.

The trail along the edge of the small creek was overgrown with a lot of underbrush and with the recent chinook the smaller branches had thawed enough to straighten out and align themselves at a perfect height to catch head-gear. The result? Branches would grab at Dad's wool toque and toss it in the air. To Dad's consternation, the hat was eventually caught on a higher branch where it stayed. Now, I don't rightly know whether that was the last straw or whether it just made a perfect target, but it was shot down...patience, at times, not being one of Dad's greatest virtues. At any rate, Dad also mentioned he'd heard the mysterious whirring sounds when he was on his way back and they'd come from the vicinity of the portage to the west.

This really worked double time on our imaginations and our thoughts turned to ghosts, possibly even the *wee-sac-hi-jack*. We'd been told this old Cree legend of a spirit that roamed the wilderness causing trickery and mischief. We'd even heard the stories of Big Foot, a big, hairy, tall beast that occasionally made an appearance across your peripheral vision but mostly caused mass speculation. These were great stories for around a campfire, but not for a young mind just getting ready for bed!

Sleep came, but not without a bit of fuss because it seemed to be a good time for an older brother to really play up these ghost and Big Foot legends. I guess we just had different views on the subject, but I was terrified and needed a good *poo-wah-gun*, the Cree word for a protector, instead of a big brother who enjoyed scaring me. I guess I just needed Mum and Dad. Eventually sleep did come, but there were a few trouble spots along the way.

Sometime during the night I recall being cold, but only for a bit, and then nothing until morning when a very mad and upset brother was wailing on me and yelling for Mum. Apparently, being cold, I had pulled on my parka to cover up, but instead of wearing it normally, had put it on by shoving my feet and legs through the sleeves. It made quite a picture! But that wasn't near the half of it. Due to, I'm sure, those last few brotherly digs at me before sleep—so I cannot be held totally responsible—I had peed the bed. It was good and soaked, and of course Clarence was not impressed whatsoever! Funny way for my poo-wah-gun to help! I guess I did get even, but I suppose the only one who really saw the humour in it all was Dad because he had less to do with the whole situation.

I was that morning's alarm clock, so the day got under way. Dad headed out onto the trapline and because of my input—or rather, my output—Mum had her day planned as well. Clarence wasn't talking to me at the moment, and so the day passed uneventfully and a bit quieter than usual. That was the last time I ever soaked the bed—and the last time Clarence deliberately tried to scare his younger brother! Though we did get bunk beds after that.

When Dad arrived home he had a full load of fur; he'd had a great day. He also told us the mystery of the strange noise we'd heard was solved. He'd met up with George and learned the whirring sound had come from George's newly acquired snowmobile from Anton. Just inside the portage, the throttle had stuck on the snowmobile, which then raced off, stopping only after a head-long plunge into a giant spruce tree! The impact smashed the hood, broke the muffler and damaged the starter. George had taken the starter assembly off and wrapped a manual pull cord around the crank to start the motor instead. He became very efficient at wrapping the long cord and pulling it to spin the motor and this was the distinctive sound we'd heard on the chinook wind that day. We marveled at how fast George could wrap and pull the cord so quickly!

Dad said it wasn't a real good visit, however, as George was visibly upset and made mention of the fact he'd seen Dad's snowshoe tracks from when he'd scouted Philion Lake. Although it had nothing to do with George and his agreed-upon area, still he felt it was an intrusion and obviously was disturbed by it. Dad surmised it was a combination of things that had gotten George's dander up: troubles with the snowmobile and then finding out wolves had invaded his line, feeding on all the fur caught. And maybe he was even a little bushed, a term used for someone who'd stayed too long in solitude. Could be he'd just had a bad day, too.

Dad had taken his leave, mentioning that Frank would be coming in shortly and that it was very likely we would travel out with him. Dad suggested it would be a good opportunity for George to go out as well—he'd have a ride right into Big River.

midwinter

It was now mid-winter and we could sense the season was starting to change. The days were getting longer and the sun gave off a good degree of warmth, a very welcome embrace. Some afternoons I would just stand there and soak it all in. And with this change in the air, Dad and Mum were now talking seriously about gathering in the trapline and organizing a trip out on Frank's back-haul. After this trip we would gear up for spring trapping. Dad planned to trap muskrat and beaver on Smoothstone Lake where the Philion River came in.

The next few days were extremely busy, for Dad especially; he was taking advantage of thc longer days and was going hard. It was still cold out, although once the sun reached its highest point the temperature warmed considerably—a huge relief from the long, cold, winter days. Dad was usually well away before sunrise and at about tea break that extra boost of warmth from the sun was sure appreciated. The fire was always more than just a place to boil the teapot, used as it was to dry clothing damp from walking the trail. And, as always, there was a great sense of security in sitting around a campfire. Strange as it may seem, it's like a temporary home away from home and even days later when you pass by, it beckons like an old friend. It's like you left a part of yourself there—and in a way you have, with quiet thoughts of past, present and the future.

This time of winter is what we called the "prelude" to spring, a time of year generally wind-free with clear blue skies, when it's still relatively cold enough, though, that both footwear and snowshoes remain dry. It's a time of year when you've weathered the coldest of days and are now acclimatized to winter. The rigours of the trapline become second nature, and you perform your duties with a minimum of effort, unlike the start of the season with its many trials that come with a lot of aches and pains. It's a grand time to be at home in the wilderness, a time when you really appreciate what nature has to offer.

Dad completed the task of removing all the sets from the long hauls, which included both parts of Big Mahigan. There were three other lines still out, but we would keep the trapping local, extending only to the perimeter of our home lake. The short trapline around the lake would bring in enough while we readied ourselves for the spring move to Smoothstone. Once nature decides it wants spring, it doesn't take long before the snow and ice honour the fact, and we wanted to be ready to pull out of Mahigan with little delay. But winter wasn't over yet and could still throw a punch or two.

Dad decided to go and pull the traps and snares on the longest line left. The run was at the northwest end of the lake where a small snowshoe trail carved and wriggled its way through a forest of tall poplar trees. These bare-limbed trees looked like ancient skeletons without their covering of leaves. Small clumps of alder willow spread throughout the area were completely dwarfed among these monarchs of the forest. It was a short walk through this higher ground and after crossing the bluff you entered a dark, foreboding part of the trail, thick with evergreens. At first there were a few monstrous spruce trees, then the land gradually sloped towards smaller spruce trees and thick undergrowth. It looked like the snowshoe trail went through a tunnel and carried on for some distance before the bush started to give way to a clearing ahead.

This trail led into a huge muskeg, a marshy flatland almost free of trees except for a few small bluffs. These mounds held a few straggly trees of spruce and tamarack, and they looked completely out of place standing in the immense expanse of bog. These small groups of trees were a distant reminder that islands had once dotted this area until time slowly closed the gap and algae turned the one-time lake into stagnant waters, which grew over into muskeg. This massive muskeg stretched out almost three-quarters of a mile in width and about a mile in length. In summer it was firm enough to walk on the peat-moss hummocks and grassy banks that lined the perimeter. Winter was another story. The clearing made a great place to trap and hunt as well. Game trails established over many years were plentiful and came out at regular locations all along this clearing.

Dad returned just short of dark with a good catch, mostly small fur, and he managed to bring everything back in one load, which included all the trapping accessories; another run closed for the season.

Clarence and I ground up some moose meat during the course of the day; Mum wanted to make meatloaf for the evening meal. At this point we were again getting low on our staples and there wasn't a whole lot to choose from, but as always, Mum managed to scratch something together. Along with the meatloaf was fresh bannock that had miraculously cooled down without us boys having at it first. The meatloaf was done in plenty of time for supper and when Dad arrived we sat down straight away. Instant potatoes and gravy completed the meal. The potatoes came out of a box and water was added to make it the right consistency; although a bit bland, it was a dry good that became familiar to us since it kept for long durations in the bush. All in all, we didn't mind and it tasted just fine, especially with a bit of margarine on top. Mum cut a few pieces of bannock and put them inside the little oven to reheat, then to our surprise, she set a small tin of strawberry jam on the table. How she'd kept it hidden is a mystery, but we were glad for it because having gone without for so long, it tasted even better. Hot bannock and strawberry jam washed down with a cup of light tea mixed with plenty of sugar and powdered milk was just about the best way to end the day.

As Mum cleaned up the dishes and sorted out her kitchen, Dad went about the business of cleaning fur. There was quite a number of squirrels, a few weasels and, on this final run, a small fisher as well. While he was stretching out the last of the squirrel pelts, Dad shared his trip into the big muskeg country.

It was always a joy, he told us, to walk through those tall stands of poplars; they were like kings of the forest—tall, straight and proud. And then continuing on past the thick evergreens and out to the edge of the clearing, approaching the open muskeg, he slowed down, keeping a constant lookout for anything that moved. Today had been one of those days when he was privileged to see wildlife, and just north of Dad's trail along the edge of the treeline he'd spotted a cow moose in the process of crossing the large opening. There were a lot of fresh tracks where the trail came out so there was a good chance the moose had been spooked by Dad's approach, although it seemed to be in no great hurry and ambled slow-like as it crossed the large frozen bog. Moose have a gangly gait to them and this one's was even more noticeable being heavy with calf, which made her look like she was rolling from side to side. Her long legs made travelling in the deep snow relatively easy and it wasn't long before she disappeared into the thick undergrowth on the far side.

At this point it was time to boil the teapot and have a bit of lunch. It may seem insignificant to others, but for a trapper on the trail it's quite special when, no sooner than the campfire's going, a feathered visitor shows up out of the blue. Grey Jay, Canada Jay and whiskey-jack are some of the names associated with this friendly companion to the outdoorsman. Usually one will show up first to test the waters, and then soon after its mate will make an appearance. Dad always left a piece of bannock for them as a thank you of sorts for the pleasant company they brought, chirping and chattering in between grabbing ahold of any morsel of food available to them. Once they get a beakful, they store the food in one of many crevices among the trees, then it's back for more. Many times this small bird has entertained a lonely trapper, and quite possibly kept them from going mad. A number of years later, Elmer Attleson, an old friend of the family, called them "camp-robbers," but always followed that up with a chuckle.

After a final cup of tea, it was time to check the last leg of the run. The gear was stored back in the packsack and the leftover remnants of the meal were left for the pair of whiskey-jacks. The trail led towards the north for a short distance to where there were a few fox and squirrel sets. All the snares were removed and returned to the packsack on the upward trek. There was a good selection of small fur and on one of the very last fox sets, the fisher had been caught. It was a small male with thick black fur—a great addition to the inventory and a very good way to end the run.

Dad noticed a large raven flying overhead and then another. These large black scavengers of the northland stay all winter and feed on any carrion they can get ahold of and are oftentimes a real menace to a trapper if they get to your catch before you do, hence, the importance of checking your line on a regular basis. These large birds fly tremendous distances in search of food and are close at hand on any trapline, making their rounds on a regular basis. When the day wears on and light starts to wane, they make a beeline back to their nests for the night. At times it looks like they don't know what direction to go in and seemingly criss-cross the sky, but eventually, they all find a place to spend the night.

The day was wearing thin by the time all the sets had been gathered, and with the ravens showing signs of going to roost, it was high time for Dad to do the same. Walking home was relatively easy as the line had been completed on the way in and the back-trail was excellent. It was a straight run, and even with the amount of fur he carried there was no slowing Dad down. So it wasn't too long before he'd left the forest for the shoreline of Little Mahigan, and home was just around the corner.

We were late getting to bed. A combination of things, I suppose: excitement due to the upcoming trip, a change in the weather causing aching bones, and maybe for us boys, the desire for a little more of that strawberry jam! At any rate, by the time we were in bed the wind had come up. We could see that it had started snowing by the huge snowflakes bouncing off the window glass, the flakes illuminated briefly in the light of the gas lantern inside. According to the forecast heard over the radio earlier, Dad figured we might be in for one of those surprises that crop up from time to time as winter does its very best to hang on.

When morning arrived we could see that it was going to be one of those days where any outside activities would have to be limited to within the home boundary. It was a whiteout; the whole lake looked like one large, blank sheet. We were hard-pressed just to see the edge of our clearing. It was a good feeling to know the majority of the trapline had been pulled in and not have to break trail and reset everything, though there were a few small items still to look after. Once the wood box was filled and the water barrel topped up, we hunkered down to wait out the late winter storm until it blew itself clear.

Most of the afternoon we had our own things to keep us occupied and there wasn't a lot of communication going on, but it was quite loud inside anyway due to the howling wind. Every time a gust raged around the cabin or across our little clearing it seemed like the cabin complained, the structure creaking and grumbling, with the odd snap from a drying check on one of the cabin's log walls. When a log dries it shrinks and at times will audibly split the full length of the log or tree. The old forty-five, our barrel stove, protested the extra draw created by the passing wind and loudly moaned and sometimes even whistled as it sucked air past the damper. It was times like this that I could really believe in the boogie-man and in spirits of times past.

Mum made some fresh bannock and once it had cooled down enough to eat, she cut it into thin slices and set it on the table, along with a fresh cup of tea and more of the precious strawberry jam—the supply of which was already depleting rapidly. We sat down for an afternoon snack while the storm raged on throughout the rest of the day. Although the snow diminished somewhat it was still severely cold and windy out, and with no reason for us to be anywhere else but inside, we turned in for the night.

a trapper's calendar

The next day was breathtaking. The storm had passed and left in its place a gorgeous and brilliant winter wonderland. Not a lot of snow, surprisingly, just enough to refresh the whole area—the snow that had fallen on the trees blew off in short order but still left a good six inches on the ground to contend with.

After soaking in the beauty of nature's majestic display, it was time to dig out. First off, we had to replenish the never-endingly hungry wood box and thirsty water barrel, both of which were now—distressingly—showing signs of nearing the bottom. Outdoor chores were a lot of fun after a snowfall, mainly because of all the horsing around we did.

And there's something special about making new tracks in the freshly fallen snow, so chores lasted a bit longer due to one or two stops to make snow angels—although it soon turned into a competition of who could make the best one, which, of course, my brother won as we were playing by his rules. But hey, he was my older brother and knew best, which he politely told me at the top of his voice! Anyway, the chores did get done and then it was out to the fish net.

We always looked forward to pulling out the net since we could never be certain what the catch would be. The net had remained in this spot throughout the winter and the perimeter of the basin hole had slowly developed into a huge wall of ice around three sides; the accumulation of snow and ice from clearing the hole resembled a small fortress. Today wasn't much different from the many pulls we'd done before as far as the number of fish caught. There were a few whitefish, northern pike and some rough fish—enough for a couple of good feeds. However, today we didn't draw the net back under the ice. Instead, Dad and Mum, one on each side of the net at the anchor-hole, neatly piled the weights and floats as the net was pulled from the lake. This was the last day we'd use it. Once the net was rolled up, the anchor lines drawn and the running line wound up, the fish were loaded in a tub on the sleigh and hauled off home. Back at camp, Mum cleaned the fish and prepared them for our meal. Meanwhile, Dad stored all the fishing gear in the small shack-tent. The net was hung on a pole and thoroughly dried before boxing it for later use.

The midday meal was fresh whitefish and hot bannock, a meal that never seemed to lose its appeal. Maybe it was the way in which it was cooked or maybe it was just plain seasoned with a true taste of outdoor spice, but for whatever reason you couldn't beat it and it remains one of our favourite meals. After lunch, Dad made one last run for the day. He started out on the west shore and circled the edge of the lake until he reached the small river at the north end where the last of the traps were. From that point he made straight for the cabin.

From our vantage point we watched Dad's return with interest, noting the little wisps of snow tossed up by his snowshoes with each step, and wondering how he was able to keep his trail so straight. When he got back and was taking off his snowshoes we asked him about it. Dad told us that he lined himself up between two trees on the shoreline and kept them in his line of sight as he walked, allowing him to keep to a straight path. There was no fur caught today, most likely due to the storm we'd just had.

The sun was getting higher now with each passing day and the warmer temperatures put a glaze on the surface of the snow, creating a brilliant reflection of blinding white. You had to shield your eyes to protect yourself from becoming snow blind. We didn't have sunglasses so we improvised, using strips of cloth wrapped around our heads with just enough of a slit to see through, and this was adequate for the brightest part of the afternoon. The reflection also caused another springtime phenomenon: the spring tan. We all got quite dark, although Dad was more windburned than tanned and still frostbitten from a few of the colder days already past.

The season was changing and the birds knew it. Chickadees sang flat out to let us know in no uncertain terms that spring was here, the birds chirping steadily as they fluttered in and out among the trees, feeding. The pair of whiskey-jacks that claimed the area around our cabin started paying us regular visits again after a brief period of absence; more than likely they'd been attending a nest and now that the young were hatched it was a full-time job scrounging for food to satisfy their ravenous appetites.

Even though the hours of sunlight were getting longer there still wasn't enough time in the day to get everything accomplished. Being busy made the time whiz by and next thing we knew nightfall had arrived and it was time for bed. Sleep came slowly as we lay there listening to an owl *hoot-hooting* into the night, enjoying an evening of no wind, mild weather and clear skies.

We woke up in a hurry when Dad yelled "Come and get it!" At first we weren't sure what "it" was. But only for a moment, then we could smell the sweet aroma of fresh, homemade hot cakes. Dad repeated, "Better come and get them while they're hot!" We sure didn't have to be told a third time! Knowing this was the last of the ingredients until we could get to a store made them taste even better.

After breakfast, Dad left to pull the last of the line. The final run was along the spring, and it wouldn't take very long to retrieve the last of the sets. It was unlikely they would be successful because of the amount of snow cover on them, but you never knew. Regardless, they had to be pulled before we left.

Meanwhile, Mum took advantage of the beautiful spring day and started washing clothes. This was bittersweet to us boys as it meant quite a few trips to the water hole, but we did appreciate the clean clothes and once we were in the swing of it the chore usually turned into some game that Clarence would dream up, like seeing who could haul water the fastest or who could fill the pails the quickest. Either way, I usually lost and I *always* wound up wet!

Dad returned later than usual. After checking the line and finding to his chagrin that his prediction of not catching any fur was indeed accurate, he'd decided to go see if George was home. And he was. They'd had a good visit and thoughts of their last meeting in the portage were set aside, or maybe it was just spring and time to get on with other things. George was getting his gear ready for the trip out to Big River as well; he'd follow along when we left. After a cup of tea and catching up with each other's latest news, Dad bade him farewell. "It was good to see George again," he told us.

We spent the rest of the day properly storing all the trapping equipment and repairing any gear that required fixing. Most of the trapping accessories were placed in the small shack-tent, while items needed at Smoothstone were kept near the door for easy access. The day ended when all the supplies were stored and the fading sun gave a sense of finality to the winter trapping season. We celebrated with a meal of ground moose meat patties, along with instant potatoes and gravy. "Northern News" sent out a number of messages to trappers on the line. Along with the messages, the host announced that fur pelts were in high demand and bringing in excellent prices. We were really encouraged by this good news and eagerly looked forward to what our fur would bring. We were ready to go and now it became a waiting game, wondering exactly when Frank would arrive with the material for his fishing camp.

And so the anticipation grew.

The next couple of days brought more warm weather and signs of snow starting to settle and even melt some, especially under large trees with huge branches and where the sunlight hit directly. And then we heard our first crow. *Kawww-kawww! Kawww-kawww!* At this sure sign of spring, we all dashed out for a better look. A real bushman's tradition and a regular phenomenon each year is waiting for the first spring birds to arrive. The crow, an all-black smaller relative of the raven that migrates south for the winter, is usually one of the first to return. Once you hear the tell-tale *kawww-kawww!* you know that winter is indeed on its way out. Folks who spend their winters in the bush relate to this small black scavenger as the true sign of the change in seasons and then it becomes a regular routine to search the skies for the next returning bird.

Trappers, as a rule, don't leave a lot of notes behind, and if they *do* mark down something of interest it's usually on a homemade calendar. Many trappers' calendar notes would read something like: "Seen first crow. Seen first eagle. Squirrels have gone nuts mating—can't blame them ... long winter! Seen first sea-gull. Ducks and geese are here. Seen a robin and a Blue Heron." And now that our first crow had arrived, we started our own countdown as well.

It was about mid-afternoon on the third day when we heard the *clippity-clop* and *jingle-jangle* of the horse team before they rounded the point. After pulling up, Frank covered the two horses with thick blankets and tossed them a bale of hay to chomp on. Then Frank was kindly dragged inside for the customary tea and a hot meal. While Mum put on a bowl of hot stew for our guest, Dad and Frank caught each other up on all the news from the outside world and the trapline respectively. Frank's wife Rosella had sent a few candy bars in for us boys and we didn't need to be asked twice whether we wanted one! Although Frank teased us a bit, saying that we probably didn't like sweets anyway.

At any rate, the conversation led to Frank's trip in and when he was going back. Frank said the portage was fine; the amount of snow hadn't slowed down the horses in the least. George had made several trips out to the landing at Smoothstone with his snowmobile and the trail was hard where he'd been, but most of the trail led down the centre of the portage and the sleigh straddled George's path, making the horses' work a bit harder.

Nonetheless, it had been a good trip in. Frank said he'd drop off some material and a bit of equipment at his fishing camp, then overnight and pick us up the following morning. After the meal, Frank made his way back to the lake and uncovered the animals. With a flick of the reins, they were off. The two horses were quite refreshed and eager to go after their brief respite and made short work covering the rest of Little Mahigan Lake in their enthusiasm. We could tell that both our parents were looking forward to seeing friends and relatives, and the atmosphere was charged with a sense of electricity for the rest of the day.

Dad also left shortly after our guest's departure to let George know we would be leaving the following day. He hadn't gone very far when he met George coming up the lake to see us; George had seen the tracks in the portage and wanted to know when we were leaving. Dad invited him to have a meal with us. Clarence and I were always excited to see George and had already adopted him as a grandpa, and it was clear he thought of us as his own family as well. George told us he'd get all of his necessary gear and fur together and close up camp tonight. He would leave ahead of us at first light. He also said he was pulling out of Mahigan for good and would be relocating to La Ronge where there was a job prospect of pulling B-trains by Caterpillar north to one of the mines. It was almost certain he would be hired. We were sad that George wouldn't be returning to Mahigan and that this part of his life would now be behind him, but Dad comforted us, saying that it was okay, that people moved on and that we would see him again. It was more than likely we would be doing the same at some point.

As soon as George left, we tidied up the last few things before bedtime. Tucked in, we listened to our parents talk long into the night about how long we should stay out and if there would be enough time to make it to La Ronge for a visit with Mum's side of the family. They agreed that ten days should be sufficient time to do all the business as well as make a quick trip to La Ronge. Even if it took a few extra days, it wouldn't be too critical; it was still early enough in the year and the melt had yet to begin in earnest.

And so the night wore on; the murmuring of voices diminished and the candlelight dimmed until all was still and quiet.

time to go

Morning brought with it renewed enthusiasm. By the time Clarence and I cleared our eyes, breakfast was being served. The one-room cabin was warmed thoroughly to every corner and the gas lantern, lit for extra light on this special occasion, hissed persistently. Tea was already hot and steeped, and we had bacon and eggs for breakfast, freshly dropped off by Frank the previous day. There was no need for us to be told and it wasn't long before we were at the table with one of our most treasured items in hand—a fork!

After that great meal, we went in all different directions. Mum washed and put away the dishes, then made lunch for the trip out. Dad started carting out all the necessary gear and items we were taking with us. Some of the items would be temporarily left at the old cabin at Selenite Point and the rest we would take with us. The bundles of fur were the last items to be taken down to the lake. Dad noted that there were several of these bundles; we sensed a bit of pride in his voice and we were proud of him as well. It was good to see him take a moment to recognize the accomplishments gained by all his hard work over the months of the winter season.

Soon we could see the horse team rounding the northeast point and watched as they quickly made their way across. And shortly, Queeny and Tippy pulled up in fine fashion, white cylindrical columns of air puffing out each time they blew through their nostrils. Although it was the start of spring season, the weather was by no means showing it today—it was bitterly cold out. Frank and Dad loaded everything in the sleigh and packed it in good and tight while still leaving enough room for us to ride too. Clarence and I decided it was like Santa's sleigh—and it was, in its own way.

It wasn't long before we were ready to go. The last thing brought down to the lake was a few small stones that had been heated over the stove, then wrapped in canvas and a blanket. These were placed on the floor of the sleigh to warm our feet. With one last look around the cabin to make sure that everything was secure, we were off!

As we approached the portage we saw that George had already gone on ahead, so we pressed on. There would be no one at Mahigan for some time now, and knowing it, we felt a loss—but it was short-lived because we were now inland and the trail absorbed our interest. The sleigh jolted back and forth and on more than one occasion bounced around like a bucking bronco, usually when it crossed George's snowmobile trail, which seemed to happen quite often. Clarence and I thought it was fun until the novelty wore off, and eventually we found no humour at all in pitching to and fro. There were a few spots along the trail where it followed the incline of a hill and the tilt of the sleigh left very little room to manoeuvre—thoughts of overturning must have been in more minds than just ours because Dad hopped off and steadied the vessel as it made its way down to flatter terrain. Clarence didn't seem to mind, but I was certainly scared enough during this ordeal, although in hindsight, my fear was likely caused by the fact that my brother was screaming in my ear telling me this was surely the end and tipping over was almost guaranteed. Once we were past the hill, the journey became mundane and we settled in, rocking with the ride.

The horses plodded along and we made good time. We were just past the halfway point in the portage when we came upon George. He had a large fire going and a pot of hot tea on. He'd had snowmobile trouble and stopped to repair it. The fuel line to the carburetor had frozen tight and had to be thawed out. He'd been about ready to leave when he heard us coming, so he stoked up the campfire and made sure there would be hot tea for everyone, knowing we could use a warm up. This was a welcome sight—we were feeling the cold and it was great to get off the sleigh for a bit to stretch, move around and regain some circulation, not to mention warm up at the fire.

We didn't stay long and after a quick cup of tea it was back on the trail, for we had some distance to travel before the day was done. It's amazing how animals react after a bit of rest. It was like the horses had regained all their energy and just couldn't wait to get going. Dad told us horses behaved this way when they knew the next destination was home. Clarence and I pondered this bit of information and agreed that it made sense, though our sense of *home* was currently in the process of being displaced and we wondered what our next home would be like. But we were glad the horses had a home to be excited about, and we were also glad they were taking us there. The horses kept up a lively gait and we soon found ourselves coming out onto Smoothstone.

After leaving the portage, we made a round-about circle away from the mouth of the Mahigan River and over to the cabin on Selenite Point where Frank had parked his truck. When we pulled up, Dad immediately went to work preparing a fire in the old cabin. Frank unhitched the horses and wiped them down before covering them and releasing them into a small, crudely-built corral where they pastured when not at their main place. He busted open a couple of bales of hay for them to feed on.

Soon after, the small wood stove held a good roaring fire and warmed the small cabin enough for us to start peeling off a few layers of winter wear. It was sure nice to feel the heat, making us realize how cold it had been outside—a good reminder that winter could still pack a punch. A warm cabin, hot tea with plenty of powdered milk and sugar, and things were okay.

Mum scurried about the cabin, tending to us boys and getting lunch on the go. The men finished off their tea and went outside to get Frank's truck started. Mum had just finished setting out the mid-afternoon meal of hot stew and bannock sandwiches when we heard the roar of the truck outside. And by the sounds of the revving the men were obviously delighted with their success. It's amazing how wonderful a hot meal tastes after working up an appetite out in the cold. The day's chill made the meal even tastier and the food was devoured with gusto.

Though our bellies were full and we were warm, there was still Smoothstone Lake to cross and no time to relax.

a season ends

We closed up camp and made sure everything was secure before pulling out. We made for a strange-looking train, George with his snowmobile pulling a toboggan full of personal possessions, Frank in his truck loaded down with gear and empty drums. And then there was us, following along behind with Dad driving the team of horses. A mixed convoy to be sure. It was the only time I recall Dad having anything to do with horses.

It was late afternoon by the time we arrived at Frank and Rosella's home on the southwest shore of Smoothstone. Rosella, Louie and Barb were standing outside and greeted us as we pulled up to their front door. Frank and George had made better time and were well ahead of us, so Rosella was prepared for our arrival with lots of hot coffee, tea and moose stew. The aroma of fresh bread immediately tickled our senses and soon we were seated at the small table devouring the meal with ravenous appetites brought on by the long, cold trip. The wind had picked up about halfway across the lake, which made the last leg of the journey unpleasant, but after a hot meal in a warm, cosy cabin the cold was all but forgotten.

Frank's truck on Smoothstone Lake

And there was a surprise! Rosella had made homemade peanut butter to put on the hot bread. This was a first! Both Clarence and I made short work of a few slices of fresh bread and also managed to clean up the peanut butter—we liked how it stuck to the top of our mouths. Meanwhile, Dad had started our half-ton truck and it was now warm enough and ready to go. The truck was loaded with everything we needed for our trip out. George took everything in his possession with the exception of the snowmobile, which he gave to Dad; we would use it to take us back to Selenite Point upon our return. George thought it was almost ready for retirement anyway.

With a farewell wave to our hosts we headed for Big River.

George insisted on riding in the back to make more room for us and would not hear the protests from Mum and Dad. He wrapped himself in his sleeping bag and Dad covered him with a canvas tarp he had in the back of the truck. It was all that could be done to make George comfortable. Dad stopped several times on the way in to check on him and each time everything was fine.

The road into Big River was no different than when we had travelled it last fall—it was still rough as ever, though the dust had been replaced by a thin layer of packed winter snow. There were no further delays and we arrived in the small community

Louie (oldest son of Frank and Rosella Schoegle), Rosella, us boys (me with my tongue out!), and little Barb Schloegle

safely, although by this time it was real late. We dropped George off at the hotel; he'd find his own way from there. It would be several years before we came in contact with George again.

Dad didn't want to barge in on the relatives at this hour so we stayed at the hotel as well. Once booked in it was straight to the room. After a quick inspection the bed drew us boys like a magnet and it wasn't long before we lay there gazing at the four walls that made up the small room. There was one double bed and a fold-up, a single bed that Mum set out for us. Meanwhile, Dad invited George downstairs to celebrate their season of trapping and the adventures of the past winter. Once we were tucked in, we remembered nothing until the following morning when we were awakened—it was time to check out. Dad and Mum were raring to go, the desire to get the winter's catch sold spurring them on. After checking out we walked over to a small café where we had a breakfast of sausage and eggs and a generous amount of hash browns. The bakery-cut bread—not to mention a thick layer of jam—fascinated us to the extent that we had several slices of toast,.

There were two general stores in Big River at the time: O.P. Godin's and the Red & White. Breakfast over, we headed over to the Red & White general store to sell the fur. We followed Dad inside and watched as the store owner went through the process of grading all the pelts. Starting with the smaller furs, the fur buyer counted each type and made a note, then moved on to the larger pelts and went through the same procedure. He took a little longer with the larger ones, shaking the pelt to fluff out the fur and then brushing his hand across it to feel its thickness until he'd completed all the pelts and his final notation. It was really quiet while all the tallying was being done. Instead of telling Dad what the total was, he handed Dad a piece of paper with a figure showing what the whole lot was worth. Dad must have been pleased as a huge grin spread across his face and with a nod he accepted the price. Deal done, the agreement was sealed with a hearty handshake. Not all these transactions benefited us; there were times over the years these deals were heartbreaking—but this one was good!

Meanwhile, Mum was going through the shelves in the clothing part of the tiny store, looking at what was new and trendy. A scarf set caught her eye and she set it at the counter for purchase, a good way to start the holidays. Dad wanted to see family before we left for La Ronge, so from the store it was straight over to visit his sister Priscilla and her husband Clarence, as well as his brother Ben and his wife Marie. It was always great to stop in and visit cousins and see their new toys. After a few hours of catching up with the family news, we made our departure. We made another stop at the Red & White before leaving Big River, and Clarence and I purchased a pop and candy bar out of our small change—ten cents for a bottle of pop and five cents for a candy bar—and with that we were satisfied and ready for the long trek to La Ronge where we would visit family and friends.

The road trip took us through the city of Prince Albert. Once we'd arrived in the city, we decided to spend the night before travelling any further and booked into the Avenue Hotel. It would be nice to do some shopping and the variety of merchandise at hand was a real treat. Clarence and I had the privilege of seeing a picture show at a local theatre just a block or so down from the hotel on Central Avenue. It was called the Orpheum Theatre and to us it looked just like what most people would call Hollywood. The time passed quickly and it was real neat to spend a night in the hotel. The next morning came fast and it was soon time for the journey north. After fuelling the truck, to the brim, as Dad put it, we made one more stop—for a bucket of chicken, hooray!—before leaving.

The roads were clear with very little snow around the Prince Albert area, but as we travelled north the snow increased in depth and it soon started to look like we were in the dead of winter again. The road narrowed considerably after we passed through the Waskesiu area, and the further north we travelled, the more curves there were. Towering trees on both sides of the road made it look like we were driving down a corridor, the effect added to by the huge banks of snow on the edges of the road where the grader had pushed it aside. Sometimes we passed by open swamp that looked a bit like a snow desert, void of everything but white snow. In some places, we could see muskeg hummocks and small clumps of bush alder and willow; they looked almost forlorn out there.

Nonetheless, we carried on over the ups and downs, twists and turns, and after what seemed like an endless time of driving we arrived in Air Ronge. We continued on, though, crossing over the Montreal River bridge which separates the two communities of Air Ronge and La Ronge. At last we had arrived.

First off, we needed to find a place to stay so after a drive

Philip Chenard

Louisa Chenard

through La Ronge to take in all the local sights, we drove to a friend's place. Philip and Louisa Chenard had a house in Air Ronge. Dad had known Phil since they were children living in Big River. Dad was a bit older than Phil, but an immediate friendship had been established and they remained close friends throughout the years. Although they didn't necessarily chum together a lot, their lives paralleled each other and they had a lot in common, not just the similarity of the times, but because they were men who had chosen the life of a bushman and fully embraced the challenges that lifestyle presented with vigour and perseverance. And persevere they did, even in those times when tenacity was all that was left to hold onto.

But for now, we had time to visit and enjoy the company of family and friends, renewing old acquaintances and socializing with the outside world. This always took a bit of time, shedding the isolation of months in the bush.

And soon enough it would be time to go spring trapping...

new beginnings

The seasons in this part of world—spring, summer, fall and winter—are distinct, each one with its own noticeable and unique differences. Even now, these Northern Lakes quench your thirst when you drink from them directly. Rivers and streams still teem, full of life, especially during the spring fish run. The birds of the air and the wildlife of the land still enjoy the full freedom of a natural life in the wilderness.

There are few places left that man has not been, but we still have the privilege of going to places where no sign of man exists. Life continues and we move onward to other locations, other destinations and new beginnings.

acknowledgements

One of the greatest gifts one can have is the opportunity to give thanks. Thank you to the Lord Jesus Christ for allowing me to live in this place and time. Thank you to all those who played a part in shaping my life and to those special few who took me under their wings.

Heartfelt thanks to Mum and Dad. Dad gave me a solid foundation to build from and his teachings gave me the ability to survive; we had wonderful experiences even though he was with us for only a short time and his lessons will remain with me always. Mum instilled in me her down-to-earth values—they are the cornerstone of my life and the backbone of my adventures.

I also owe a big thank you to my brother, Clarence. We shared many of these stories together and he is always there when I need help.

Thank you and huge bear-hugs for my children: Emery, Amanda and James. Your respect for others and the support you give your mom and me make you children to be proud of.

And lastly, though first in my life, is my beautiful wife, Joan, who has never doubted and always encouraged me. Without you this book would not have been written. Thank you for sharing your life with me.

about keith olsen

Keith Olsen

I was born February 25, 1960 in the Big River Hospital, Big River, Saskatchewan, Canada to James Edward and Flora Jean Olsen. I have one older brother, Clarence Edward.

Dad's background was Scandinavian and he too was born in Big River where a good number of our relatives still live. Some of the family moved west into Alberta and British Columbia. Mum was born in La Ronge, Saskatchewan and she is a Cree Indian of the Lac La Ronge Indian Band, a First Nation People of Canada. Most of her family still live in the area.

Shortly after Clarence and I were born we moved to La Ronge. It was a small community at the time but had all the services we needed. There we got our education, sold our furs and fish, and bought the staples required for the bush. Whether we were fishing, hunting, or trapping, we called it our home base. And from there we travelled a considerable amount.

There have been summers and winters commercial fishing on Lac La Ronge Lake, and seasons spent trapping and running a hunting lodge at Mahigan Lake.

Then we moved north to an unnamed lake, later named Thompson Lake, seventy miles north of La Ronge, which became our home, and it was there we enjoyed a few wonderful years, just plain living life to the fullest as you can when you have hundreds of square miles at your disposal.

We also had the great privilege of spending a summer as a family in the Northwest Territories, after which came my career in Northern Saskatchewan working in a variety of jobs: line cutting, staking, prospecting, geophysical surveying, camp construction and commercial fishing. Growing up as I did, perhaps it's not a surprise that the North became my playground!